How to Keep Your Teenagers Out of Trouble

JAMES ELLIOTT McCALL

BOOKS FOR BETTER LIVING • CHATSWORTH, CALIFORNIA

When the voices of children are heard
   on the green
And laughing is heard on the hill,
My heart is at rest within my breast
   And everything else is still.

                    Nurse's Song
                    William Blake

CONTENTS

Preface

The purpose of this book is to keep teenagers out of trouble and to help teenagers who are already in trouble. There have been many books of this nature written by qualified men and women in the fields of psychology, sociology, and law. The difference in this book is that I specialized in *being* a troubled teenager.

I have been in jail. I've used drugs, partied with motorcycle gangs, and pulled friends through drug overdoses. Some friends didn't make it.

A year ago in March, my foster sister, Val, died from mixing whiskey and Seconal. She was twenty-one.

Billy, a friend, hung himself in an Army barracks rather than fight in Viet Nam. He was twenty.

Roy was murdered at twenty-two, and Joey went to jail for that murder at eighteen.

Somebody blew Russ off his own front porch with three blasts of a twelve-gauge shotgun a couple of years ago. Russ was twenty-three.

Dave, who I have known since he was fourteen,

just got arrested for possession of drugs, forgery, and procuring in Palm Springs.

My qualifications for this book couldn't be earned in the best university. They come from the things I have seen and lived through.

I got into a lot of trouble when I was a teenager. I'm not ashamed of it anymore, but I wish many of the experiences had never happened. Hopefully, my mistakes can do someone some good. If just one teenager listens to what I've said here, recognizes the similarities, and avoids the problems, then in a small way I will have paid back society for some of the things I've done.

I hope parents and teenagers will read this book together. The teenagers are going to laugh at some of the slang terms I've used because they may already be obsolete. They'll disagree about some of the things I've said, and I'm sure, in places, they'll think I'm out of my mind. Parents, on the other hand, won't agree with some of the solutions I offer. That's all right.

If teenagers and parents disagree with me and explain to each other why my ideas don't apply to them, they will have a better understanding of what does apply, which, in itself, will do more to keep kids out of trouble than all the advice in the world.

I've also included a number of ways parents can obtain help for their teenagers. This information came partially from my own experiences and partially from the experiences of friends.

Acknowledgments

The number of persons who have helped me assemble the information in this book is far too large for me to thank them individually, but I would like to mention a few people who were especially helpful.

Sue Mao, of the Los Angeles County Coroner's Office, provided much information about teenage death statistics and causes of death. Chalmers Smith, retired from the Glendale Police Department, supplied information about teenagers and the law.

I'd also like to thank Lee and Bruce Merrin, Faustina Orner, my publishers, and last, but far from least, my wife, Brandy.

Chapter 1

RUNAWAY!

My fifteen-year-old son has threatened to run away. Should I take this threat seriously, or is this a normal part of childhood?

The threat to run away from home is a normal part of childhood. Kids have had hassles with parents since time began, and the easiest way for a teenager to gain attention in the household is to split from it. However, times have changed, and the sentimental image of a kid carrying a brown paper bag containing his toothbrush and pajamas no longer applies. Today when a kid takes off, he could be halfway across the country before you notice he's gone. If he's warned you by threatening to split, take him seriously.

What should a parent do if a son threatens to run away?

Well, we've established that the one thing *not*

to do is ignore it. It's better to say something like, "I wish you wouldn't," than to say, "Yeah, sure kid"—which is the best way to get a teenager to prove he's got guts enough to leave.

It's also a mistake to tell him he's not allowed to run away. Restricting the teenager to his room or similar punishment amounts to the same thing.

Instead, lighten up a little, even if it's awkward to drop the parental, authority role. Try to find out why he wants to leave home. Then maybe some sort of compromise can be reached, and the problem will end there. Even if the issue isn't resolved immediately, at least the problem will be out in the open and under discussion. If he feels someone is trying to understand him, and he has hope that things are going to change at home, he won't feel pressured into taking a drastic action like running away.

How do children manage to get so far from home?

Transportation in this country is greatly improved over what it was thirty years ago, and teenagers today have access to larger amounts of money than their parents did. The price of a ticket for a 500-mile commuter plane flight can cost less than twenty dollars.

Hitchhiking is another favorite mode of transportation among teenagers. Getting beyond the city limits is the hardest part of thumbing a ride. Once on the highway, a teenager can get hundreds of miles away in a matter of hours. Other sympathetic young people are also a great aid to runaways, helping them find places to sleep, food and transportation.

Don't people pay attention to children
traveling alone?

If you're talking about traveling on airplanes, the answer is no. The airlines are in business to provide service. Service doesn't include asking customers their age. There are also many well-meaning adults with fond memories of "the time I ran away" who sometimes prove to be more helpful to runaways than are other teenagers.

Since the tragedy in Houston, where twenty-seven teenage boys were murdered, there has been more concern about runaway teenagers. Texas Governor Dolph Briscoe has started a new program called Operation Peace of Mind. Teenagers can call toll-free numbers and have messages relayed to their parents. Operators will make no effort to locate the runaways; they simply relay messages. The numbers are: 1-800-231-6946, from outside the state of Texas; 1-800-392-3352, within the state; and 524-3821, in the Houston area only. Calls are received twenty-four hours a day.

Where should a parent start looking for
a runaway?

Check with neighborhood friends and relatives first. Many runaways don't like to go out on the road alone. Nearby homes represent security and are the most likely places of refuge. If the teenager doesn't have friends in town, or doesn't turn up with one of them, widen your search to include friends or relatives in nearby towns. Don't discount the possibility that the kid might have gone clear across the country, if there are friends in distant cities.

My seventeen-year-old son left home. After checking out all the possibilities, I've drawn a blank. Where do I go from here?

Did a friend of his recently take a trip? Did your teenager ever express an interest in any particular part of the country? Was he interested in a job such as farming, ranching, racing, or sailing? If so, check in areas where those jobs are available.

Talk with the kid's friends. They may have supplied him with the name of a friend or relative to look up in another town. If so, the friend may not be helpful, but a short talk with the parents should clear that up. Other clues to his whereabouts would include any town names scribbled on scraps of paper, bus or airline schedules, a road map or well-thumbed page in an atlas, travel folders, or any other written evidence that may have been inadvertently left behind. Tear his room apart; most kids leave some clue.

Once the general area is thought to be known, what's the next step?

If there is some definite indication of where the teenager is, a parent may want to go there. If this isn't possible, he could try contacting the people the child might be staying with. If there's no definite address, a parent could prepare a circular with the teenager's description, habits, job abilities, pictures, and any other information which might be helpful. Send this to the police in the area, and ask them to check their files of juvenile arrests. The police receive thousands of these each year, but sometimes it helps them establish the identity of an uncooperative teen.

Is there any other way of locating a runaway?

It depends. If the child is under eighteen and has a Social Security Card, the Social Security Office may be able to file a tracer, assuming that the teenager is working and using his or her real name. This usually is confidential information, but, in the case of runaways, exceptions are made. Call the local office, and they'll tell you how to go about it.

Or check with the Motor Vehicles Department in the state where you think your child has relocated. If he or she has been involved in an accident, been issued a citation, or applied for a new license, they will have that information on file, and these files are public record. They will answer your letter of inquiry promptly. To obtain the local Motor Vehicles Department address, call information in the state's capital.

How soon should the authorities be notified?

Normally, a person is considered "missing" after seventy-two hours. In the case of teenagers, a report can be filed after an "absence of unreasonable length" has occurred. Most police judge this to be three hours or so. If the teenager still hasn't shown up in twenty-four to seventy-two hours, parents will be asked to come to the station and file a formal report. When the first report is phoned in, the cars in the field are notified to keep a watch out. After the formal report is filed, the information, including picture, is given to the officers and listed in the station.

...the same local law enforcement agency you would contact in the event of a prowler, whether it's the sheriff's office, highway patrol, or city police. If there is a juvenile department, their switchboard will connect you. The FBI or state police won't do anything, other than tell you whom you should have called in the first place.

I've just about given up hope of finding my sixteen-year-old myself. Should I hire a detective?

A trained, professional detective could devote all his time to the case. If the price is right, and the man has a good record, why not?

How much could a detective cost?

The price varies. All expenses, including travel, lodging, meals, etc., plus the detective's fee, are paid for by the client. This can range from $100 to $200 a day and possibly more. The average out-of-town fee is about $150 to $200 a day, plus expenses.

To locate a runaway, the total fee usually runs from $500 to $1,000. A detective often will ask for a retainer of $200 to $500 before he does anything. Make sure you are aware of all the charges: What kind of transportation will he use? Where will he stay? How much will he spend for meals each day? What is the minimum time charge, if any? How long will it take to find the child?

How does a parent find a reputable detective?

Unless a friend or family lawyer has a recommendation, you'll have to look through the phone book. To make sure the detective is reputable, check with the Better Business Bureau to see if they have any record of complaints against him. Call the county information office and find out what kind of license is required. Make sure the detective has one. Don't sign anything without showing it to a lawyer. Almost any lawyer in the phone book will take a quick look at a contract for twenty-five dollars or less. Finally, don't take the first detective in the book. Check the prices and services available of at least three detectives; then make a decision.

Don't police detectives provide this kind of service for free?

No way. The police might keep an eye out for your teenager, if they think about it, but they aren't going to look for the kid or send his description to another town or do anything else in an active effort to help. They don't have the time or staff to chase down runaways. Even in a city the size of Los Angeles, which has a police force of over 7,000 men for its 2.8 million citizens, the police have their hands full. They like to help as much as possible, but they just don't have enough men to go around.

Will taking an ad out in one of those underground papers help?

It might not hurt. There's no guarantee that any particular runaway will read it, but there's always a chance.

Should I try looking for my child in one of those areas kids seem to congregate in?

I wouldn't suggest traveling halfway across the country chasing smoke, but if you happen to live near one of these areas and you have sufficient reason to think your child is there, why not? If going there means wandering up and down the street showing other kids pictures of your teenager and asking for help, forget it. Many of these kids have problems of their own and wouldn't help if they could. Many parents have been victimized by persons who ask for a "small gratuity" in exchange for information which has proven to be completely false. If you do decide to go and look, just walk or drive around.

Our child left home a year ago. Now we have received a letter asking for money to come home. Should we send it?

It would be better if you could bring him back personally. If that's not possible, send the money. If you are in doubt about the money being used to travel home with, it's possible to purchase a nonrefundable ticket in your town and send it, or have the travel agency send it to your child. Send no more than five dollars for food expenses with the ticket.

What might my child do in the event I don't send money? How do kids live?

If their parents don't send money to them, chances are they won't come home. A kid can find a lot of friends on the street. On the coasts, there are many "no questions asked" job opportunities for teenagers who want work, and other even more illegal sources of easy cash.

Pushing dope is easy, profitable, and dangerously exciting. There's a huge demand for young girls in prostitution, topless and nude dancing, or massage parlor work. Boys are also sexually exploited, but they more often tend to engage in active crimes: burglary, purse snatching, or hold-ups.

Not all runaways turn to crime, but it is often the easiest, fastest way of making money, and it is often the way their new street associates get their money.

This is the fourth time my son has run away, then phoned for the fare to come home. Should I keep sending it?

It sounds like your son is getting a lot of all-expense-paid vacations. It's a hard decision to make, and the age and location of the child must be considered before making it. When a child has run away four times, each time using his parents' money to come home, it's time he learned a little responsibility. Still, it would be difficult to say no, in view of what might happen. I'd suggest going and bringing the child home, and finding professional counseling as soon as possible.

Does the procedure for locating runaways change when a girl leaves home?

Not really. Any runaway has the same general need to feel secure. That's why it's wise to check with friends and relatives first. A girl may need a little more security than a boy, and stay in a town where friends live and could be called upon in an emergency. Also check the YWCA or any woman's hotel in your own town and in the towns where the girl has friends. If the girl took off with a boy, the only thing to do is search for the couple in the ways already described.

My daughter ran away last week with a boy. Can I file charges against him?

The answer to that would depend on local and state laws, how old your daughter is, how old the boy is, where they went, and whether or not they got married once they got there. Your local police would probably be able to inform you how far the law can go criminally, but a lawyer would be able to answer all your questions regarding your responsibilities.

Even if charges are filed and a warrant sworn out, the boy and girl have to be found and the charges proven before anything can be accomplished. Pressing charges is likely to do little more than make you feel better.

If the laws allow, should parents file charges against the boy their daughter ran off with?

I wouldn't. First of all, many people view bringing police into private business as an act of aggression. The daughter isn't going to like it, the boy isn't going to like it, and chances are the boy's parents aren't going to be any too thrilled. If everybody remains cool and works together, it's going to be easier to figure out where the kids have gone in the first place, not to mention that the kids will feel much better if they find everybody getting along when they come home.

*Our daughter left home last year at sixteen.
Now she has called and wants us to meet her at
a restaurant for a long talk. Should we force
her to come home?*

I suppose if you had some plainclothesmen accompany you, you could force her to come home. At this point, though, I don't even think the subject should come up. It's obvious that your daughter wants to get back together with you and is even willing to make the first move. How you respond to her now will determine what happens between you in the days to come.

Take a realistic look at the situation the way it is. She's been gone a year, and I imagine she's getting along all right. If she's in trouble, perhaps she has some plan in mind. Let her talk *with* you. Try to forget what happened before she left, no matter how unpleasant, and try to view things in the here and now.

Help her if she needs it, if she asks for it, and if you can. Don't hassle her about coming home unless you want to lose her completely. By the same token let her know gently that she is still welcome.

*Should a parent allow a seventeen-year-old girl to
move into an apartment with three girl friends?*

That depends. Who are the friends, and what are they like? Do you know them and their parents? First discuss the plan with all the participants. Do they have the details worked out?

Second, for what length of time do the friends want to room together? The summer only, or the entire school year? How will the bills be paid if everyone is still going to school? And speaking of school, if you approve the idea, one of the requirements should be that all of the girls involved maintain good grades. If all the girls have a good sense of responsibility, and the entire plan has parental approval, it might prove interesting. It requires a lot of planning on everybody's part and mutual cooperation.

How can we go about squelching the issue if we still don't agree?

Well, it's obvious that if you don't agree, there is a valid reason. Explain the reasons to the girl. At seventeen, your daughter is old enough to discuss decisions with you in an adult manner. If she doesn't, then the reasons against the move are apparent.

If it's something she can change, like friends, grades, or her sense of responsibility, talk it over. Show the girl that you're willing to be reasonable. Maybe the proposed apartment is in a bad section of town, and you'd go along with the idea if it were in a different neighborhood. Be honest about your objections. If your only reason is that you would feel better if she would wait another year, tell her.

Another method of dissuading her would be to point out the problems, which are bound to come up living with other girls of her age. Where you might give your daughter a lot of leeway in cleaning the bathtub or showing up on time, other people are going to make demands and expect her to fulfill her obligations. You might even role-play to dramatize some of the potentially difficult situations.

If your daughter still insists she knows best, then you just might have to put your foot down. Do it gently, but firmly. She may even threaten to run away from home, but if you control your temper, chances are she'll listen to reason.

My daughter is seventeen and wants to spend the summer bumming around the country with two other girls. Is this something that's all right for girls to do these days?

If "bumming around" means hitchhiking from one city to the next with no destination in mind for the entire summer, no, it's not all right.

If the girls want to visit friends or relatives, sightsee, or shop in a nearby city for a week or so, and plan to travel by car, bus or train, that's another matter. Talk with the parents of the other girls and determine how much money they will need to meet expenses, and discuss with everyone involved the general itinerary. If there is overall parental approval, and the girls are responsible, then, yes, this kind of trip is OK.

My daughter and her two girl friends want to travel around the country and take their boyfriends along as protection. Is this all right?

I wouldn't recommend it. A group of six is not likely to get into trouble, but I know of one case where a seventeen-year-old girl was traveling with two nineteen-year-old guys, one of whom was her boyfriend. A dozen roughnecks in a southern state took her off into the Ozark mountains, raped her, and then gave the two boys a chance to go for a gun in the middle of a ring of shotguns. Fortunately, the guys didn't try for the gun and got off with only a serious beating. The girl's boyfriend went back to look for her and neither of them was ever heard from again. I knew the one guy who got away.

I hitchhiked across the country with my own girl friend in 1969. I didn't get beat up, and my girl didn't get raped, but there were no less than three very bad scenes we were saved from by luck alone. I'd never try it again.

Does the same hold true for boys traveling around the country?

More or less. There's less chance of boys getting raped and murdered, the Houston crimes notwithstanding, but teenage boys can still get in plenty of trouble. I think it would be all right for the boys to take a short trip, as long as they had plenty of money available for transportation, had definite destinations and plans in mind, and were smart enough not to pull anything stupid like shooting pool with guys they don't know, using drugs or drinking, or trying to mess around with any small town sheriff's daughter.

My son has run away three times, and twice he's come home and made a lot of promises. If he comes back with the same old line, should I give him to the police to keep for awhile?

The police might not want him, but you could ask. In some states, parents can bring their teen-

agers before the courts for being incorrigible. You'd have to check with the police or a lawyer to find out exactly what the procedure is in your area.

I'd suggest that both of you get professional help. It sounds like a problem for a counselor, not a cop. And don't think help is only for "crazy" people. All of us need professional guidance at one time or another.

Our son returned home after an absence of two years. He's been through God-knows-what and seems retarded. Will this condition last?

I couldn't say. You'd better get him to a doctor, and don't waste any more time thinking about it. If you don't have a family physician or can't afford a private doctor, call the county or welfare office near you. They'll refer you to a clinic.

Does having an eighteenth birthday change the laws regarding runaways?

Yes. Once a child turns eighteen, he or she is considered responsible for his or her actions and an adult in all respects, with the exceptions of buying alcohol and marrying in some states. The police automatically close the file on a runaway once eighteen, and if the teenager is picked up after that, he or she only faces the charges for which he or she was arrested. The parents are not notified, unless it's requested.

However, a parent can refile an adult missing person report, and the police will carry on from there. If a teenager is still missing at the time of an eighteenth birthday, parents should contact the law enforcement agency with which the original report was filed for further instructions.

Should the police be notified if a runaway returns home? Can't they file charges against a teenager?

They can if they want to. When a kid comes back home, the police usually like to talk with the teenager and his parents. If the kid came home of his own accord, and the situation in the home is healthy, there probably won't be any further action. If the teenager has a hostile attitude, the police can file a petition, and guidance counseling may be suggested or ordered by the court.

If there are severe problems at home, the child can be kept at juvenile hall until a foster home is found, or he may even be sent to youth camp. If parents don't agree with the position of the police, of course, they are free to get a lawyer and object in court.

Is there any best way to keep my child from running away in the first place?

That will depend. Different life-styles dictate different values.

In my own case, I left home at fifteen, with my mother's full knowledge and consent, to see the attractions of this nation. On the day I left home, a man named Richard Speck murdered seven women in Chicago, and things haven't been the same since. The country isn't safe for teenagers to roam, but the desire of young people to enjoy life hasn't changed.

The teenage years are extremely difficult as

most of us can recall. The most important way to get through to teenagers is by trying to understand them and keeping the lines of communication open. Problems must be brought up and discussed. That means *talking together*. If a teenager can discuss his changing problems and emotions, the pressure to leave home won't be so great.

If the teenager expresses an interest in travel and adventure, this can be arranged with parental supervision and assistance: a short sightseeing trip to the state capital, a men-only camping trip, a weekend at a folk music festival. Or perhaps there are inexpensive school or church group excursions to provide the needed outlet and escape for the teenager.

It's important that the family do things together—as a family unit, in separate all-male or all-female excursions, and a son should spend time alone with his mother, a daughter, with her father.

Do things together and allow each other to be individuals with real problems and feelings.

A lot of teenagers aren't going to agree with some of my opinions, and that's great, if they can point out where I'm off base in my thinking as it applies to their situation. It means you'll be talking and exchanging ideas—*living* together. That keeps a family whole.

Chapter 2

DROPPING OUT—OR IN

I have a choice of sending my child to public or parochial school. Which is better?

That's a question I can't answer. If you are interested in having your child's education include religious instruction, parochial school is an excellent way of obtaining it. I'd talk to counselors or other administrators at both public and parochial schools before making a decision. I'd also take my child's desires into consideration before deciding.

What about private schools? Are they better than public?

They can be. Again, the decision should be made with the child's interests in mind. Will the child be separated from friends? Will he have to commute a great distance? Both public and private schools should be investigated thoroughly before any action is taken. Some private schools offer certain benefits: The classes are smaller, the teachers may be better, and they may have areas of intensified study in certain subjects, especially in preparation for college. But because a school is private is no guarantee of excellence. Another factor to consider, of course, would be the tuition. Can you afford private school?

We are moving to another state this fall. Will our children be held back a grade?

That would depend on the standard operating procedure of the educational system in the new state. In some states this is the policy; in others, it is not. The best thing to do, if the problem concerns you, is to check with the school board in the town you are moving to. Explain to them that you don't want your children held back. In all probability they will try to help arrange things to your satisfaction. If not, there's always private school.

One thing to consider is the reason for holding the child back. Generally, it's to reorient him to the different method of education in the new city. By reviewing the same subjects he has less pressure in school at a time in his life when he will have to make a lot of adjustments to a new environment and new friends.

Our child had good grades all through junior high. Now that she's in high school, she seems to be having a problem adjusting. It shows up at report card time. Is this normal?

More or less. When a girl enters high school

she is exposed to a more sophisticated world of social awareness and increased responsibilities. For some kids, this adjustment isn't easy. The childhood urges are pulling heavily in one direction, and the adult urges in the other. Talk with the child's adviser or counselor. If the situation doesn't improve, professional help may be needed.

Are school counselors professional in this area?

Not always. Unfortunately we spend millions of dollars each year on defense and run our schools on a shoestring. Quite often, the counselors have not had specialized training in adolescent development. They are teachers, who have taken on the extra responsibility of general counseling. If your school is fortunate enough to have a trained school psychologist on its staff, make an appointment. If not, the school should have information available regarding tutors and therapists. Or perhaps your family doctor can refer you to a clinic staffed by professional counselors.

My son is resentful, disrespectful, and generally rebellious about everything. Is this typical of a 16-year-old, or is it a symptom of deeper problems?

It could be either. It's normal for teenagers to express these particular traits. It reminds me of the story about the young man who, at sixteen, thought his father was a fool. At twenty-one, he was amazed at how much the old man had learned in just five years!

The important thing is not the rebelliousness,

but how the boy expresses it. If he channels it into drugs or delinquency, then you're in for trouble. It's a difficult period for parents. Your son is going to view your help as prying and bossiness.

Keep talking to him, and try to put up with it.

The rebelliousness will probably pass, determined to a large extent on how you handle it. This doesn't mean you should let him walk all over you. He's looking for rules to live by, but they must be presented in a way in which he will accept them. You must apply an iron hand, with a velvet glove approach. If the situation gets out of control, call in professional help.

Our 16-year-old son wants to get a tattoo. Should we agree?

In most places, parental approval is required until he's eighteen. Tell him that he'll have to wait until he's eighteen to have it done, but that you'll go with him on his birthday and pay for it if he still wants it then. That should satisfy him for awhile.

My daughter, who seems normal in all other respects, has been lifting money from my purse, I think. I hate to confront her, especially if she didn't do it. Should I try to trap her?

First, I'd make sure there was money missing and that no one else could have taken it. Count your money carefully in the future, and see if any turns up missing again. If your daughter did take the money, it is quite possible that she didn't "lift" it, but simply assumed that you wouldn't mind.

If there are more losses, ask her if she "borrowed" the amount from you when you were unavailable. If she denies it, tell her that you must have lost the money and state the amount of the loss. If she did take it and then lied to you, she'll then know that you are aware of missing money and probably won't be tempted to repeat the performance. If she denies taking money, and you later catch her helping herself to your pocketbook, give her a chance to explain.

It could be she doesn't realize she's doing anything wrong. If you find her to be the guilty party, point out that she is definitely in the wrong. If she is as normal as you think, that should end the matter.

Our child is now in junior high school and claims he needs a bigger allowance. I think that additional chores should be assigned as a condition of the deal, but my wife doesn't agree. How should the issue be settled?

The issue should be settled by a family discussion. I don't think a child should be paid to help around the house. Children should be made aware of their responsibilities at an early age, and they should feel that these responsibilities are part of being a member of the family. In most instances, chores shouldn't be assigned as a way to earn money or as a form of punishment.

My oldest boy is almost three, and he has had jobs such as picking up his own toys, helping take out small bags of trash, bringing in small objects from the market, and even helping feed his little brother. We started training him early, and now there are few tasks he watches myself or his mother do without saying, "Me do it."

Kids do deserve an allowance, not based so much on a fixed sum as on need. If there is something a child needs, he should be given the money for it, if possible. This is not to say that every whim should be granted. But a child deserves the same rights as any other member of the family. Sometimes, a child should simply be given some money to spend as he sees fit. Giving a teenager a fixed sum of money each week so that he learns how to budget himself isn't a bad idea, but be flexible.

In the case of the teenager asking for a larger allowance, if there seems to be an increased need for it and he doesn't have a casual attitude about money, grant his request, if possible. If it's not possible, explain this to him and see if there isn't a way to compromise. As far as assigning extra household work for the extra money, I'm against it, with one exception. If there's some unusual job around the house that would normally require hiring outside help, such as heavy yard work or putting in a window, hire your son instead, if he feels he would like to try the job. A lot of parental supervision will be necessary, but the results might surprise both parent and teenager.

How much part-time work should a teenager be allowed to take on?

A reasonable amount. It shouldn't interfere with health, studies, social relationships, or family responsibilities. In my senior year of high school, I worked every day from three-thirty until after midnight delivering liquor. I also flunked out of school. Obviously, the job interfered with my studies. However, there are many part-time jobs with reasonable hours—perhaps two or three hours a day after school, plus Saturdays. A part-time job is a good idea. In addition to earning money, a teenager gets experience that school alone doesn't provide; he or she learns responsibility and how to deal with adults outside the family, and gains the satisfaction earning money brings.

My son wants to work with me this summer. His mother and I would rather see him take some extra-credit summer courses. What should I do?

By all means take him to work with you. If a son wants to work with his father, and he's not allowed to, he won't have much enthusiasm for summer school. A father can teach a child a lot, both about work and about the kind of attitudes he wants his child to develop. It will be a good experience for both of you.

Are summer jobs a good idea for children?

Sure. The same reasoning applies to the validity of summer jobs as to part-time jobs during the school year.

Should I help my son with his homework?

Why not? Don't do it for him, but take advantage of the opportunity to spend time with him doing something constructive, talking over problems, and setting up study habits. You might discover he has a particular interest or ability in a subject which could flourish with some encouragement. Not only that, you might learn something yourself.

My children are studying government in school and have decided that homework is unconstitutional. Should I force them to do it anyway?

I don't like to see kids *forced* to do anything. The situation should be discussed and the reason for doing the homework explained to them. In this case, I'd suggest to the kids that they do the homework for all their classes, but have them develop the idea of it being unconstitutional and present their arguments to the government teacher. He'll either be able to prove them wrong or have to agree.

I've overheard our daughter arranging meetings with her friends to get test questions. In other words, I think she's cheating on exams. What if she gets caught? Should I talk to her?

First, if she gets caught, the outcome would depend on the rules of the school and the importance of the test. She could be expelled, would probably be suspended, and it would go down on her record. The work, of course, would be invalidated, and she may or may not be allowed the opportunity to make it up without having to take the course over.

Second, yeah, talk to her. One terrible thing about cheating is that the only person cheated is the one who is doing it. The teacher's job and pay isn't affected by student grades. But a student, who got good grades because she cheated her way through school, and a good job because of those grades, won't have the chance to cheat her employer. An employee, who didn't learn the skills to hold down a job, won't have anyone's paper to copy from.

Cheating becomes a way of life, and while a person may cheat on a exam without getting caught, trying to cheat at life won't work.

One other thing to consider: Is your daughter's desire to get good grades based on your pushing her beyond her ability?

Our teenager is having a lot of trouble with schoolwork. He doesn't do his homework and gets poor grades. Is there a way to help a kid who is flunking out?

Sometimes the reason for low grades is a poor ability in reading. You might request a meeting with his teachers and find out his reading scores on the standard reading tests. If the scores are low, the teachers might be able to suggest tutors or advise remedial reading courses.

Of course, there are other reasons for poor grades: a job, a car, a member of the opposite sex, or sports taking up too much of the teenager's time. If this is the case, find out which it is and help the kid to schedule his time. A parent's show of interest and involvement is also one of the best ways to help.

Our fifteen-year-old hates high school. He cuts classes and has even gone so far as to fake being sick. What can we do?

There's a bigger problem here than hating

school. For some reason the kid is unhappy in school. The source of his unhappiness could range from a failure to adjust socially, to difficulty in doing his schoolwork, to something as simple as a case of acne. There are kids who just can't adjust to school. If your child's counselors agree, you might want to look into continuation school.

I've heard about continuation schools, but I always thought they were for rowdies and social rejects. Are they?

I finally got my diploma from one. A continuation school is for students who, for one reason or another, can't make it in a public high school. Some of the kids there are social rejects, certainly, but others have learning problems or have been forced to drop out of high school and still want an education.

A continuation school has a small enrollment. The teachers are trained to handle a wide variety of educational problems, and they have the time to devote to individual students. The hours are adapted to accommodate students' schedules. Some classes meet every day for three or four hours in the morning or afternoon, others, on Saturday. For a lot of kids, myself included, it's the one chance they have left to make something out of themselves.

My son has never been a very good student. He is almost sixteen and wants to drop out and get a job after his birthday. Should I let him?

If it's a choice between dropping out and flunking out, dropping out brings about the same end without the hassles. It's really a shame that there isn't a way for kids to drop high school for a year and work, then have an opportunity to go back without it looking bad on their record.

Some schools have developed programs to solve this type of problem. The teenager who works part-time receives academic credits, which are applied toward graduation. In one California high school, this is called the "four/four" plan. The teenager attends class four hours each day and works four hours at a part-time job. Perhaps your son's school or another area school, which he could transfer to, has a similar program. It would be worth your while to check into it. At any rate, talk things over with the boy and his counselor at school. If he still wants to quit, let him try to get a job, and keep alive the possibility of his going back to school.

Isn't it really hard for high school dropouts to get work? My son keeps pointing to people like Walt Disney who were successful in spite of little or no formal education.

If a person has the ability, ambition, and plain guts to make something out of himself, he doesn't need a diploma or a degree to do it. However, I don't think that many people recognize exactly what a self-made man is. A self-made man doesn't start out in a good job working toward someone else's goals. He has to find something other people want or need, convince them that they want or need it, and figure out a way to provide it to them at a profit to himself. That's a lot of very hard work.

Unless a person has the makings of a Walt

Disney, all he can look forward to is a long, hard struggle up through the ranks. And if he's a high school dropout, it will be without the advantages of his better-educated competitors.

Once a kid drops out, is it hard to go back to school?

In some ways it's easy, in some ways not. The decision to go back is usually made after a teenager has had a look at the realities of earning a living and finds out he's not playing with a full deck. By this time he's got his head on straight. If he goes back to school, he knows why he's there, and he's motivated to concentrate on his studies. On the other hand, if he chooses to go back to his old high school, by now he's a year or two older than the other kids in his class, and there are bound to be problems adjusting socially.

Instead of going back to high school, he also has the option of continuation school, or if he's eighteen, he can take adult education courses to get his diploma.

My son is fourteen and very upset because he didn't make the football team. My husband is a sports nut, and his disappointment is obvious. The two of them have been uncomfortable around each other since it happened. What can I do to smooth things over?

For a start, tell your husband just like you did here. It might not be a bad idea to wait until he's in a good mood, and I'll leave getting him in a good mood up to you.

Secondly, get the two of them to do some things

together, for instance, attend a sporting event. Your husband could point out the importance of spectators to the world of sports. Your husband should also show enthusiasm for some of your son's interests. By sharing each other's interests, both of them can learn to accept and respect each other's individuality.

Are girls generally better students than boys?

According to rumor they are. Actually there isn't any reason for girls to do better in high school than boys, but, at this level, girls do seem to take studies more seriously. If a sister is making much better grades than her brother, there must be a more important reason for his poor performance than the fact that he's male.

Our son's grades have never been very good. His sister has always made straight A's. I'm sure the boy feels inferior. He doesn't even bother to try. How can we help?

The best way of helping your son would be by building up his confidence and self-esteem in the areas where he does show potential. This can be done by encouraging his abilities and interests. Compliment him on the things he does well, and underplay his sister's accomplishments a little. But be careful: Don't be a phony or lavish him with false praise. Criticize him constructively when he needs it. Also make sure his sister is aware of the situation, and solicit her support.

Our daughter wants to drop out of school. She says she can learn more by staying home with her mother and helping clean house. Is this a valid argument?

A lot of girls think their role in life will be that of homemaker and that they don't need an education. A girl can learn about homemaking from her mother, but she doesn't have to quit school to do it. There's lots of time after school, and, in fact, most schools have excellent home economics courses. And unless she expects to get married and has the boy in mind, she'll have to think of supporting herself in the future. Even marriage is no guarantee she won't have to work. She really should be advised to finish school and, in the meantime, pick up some skills she can use in the nine-to-five world of employment.

Is it unusual for a girl to want to drop gym class?

It's not unusual for anybody to want to drop gym class—for a variety of reasons. Often the teenager is embarrassed about his or her poor performance in sports or a less than beautiful body in shorts. Extremely modest girls are shy about undressing in the locker rooms. Talk it over with the girl, and if things don't work out, make an appointment with the gym teacher to get to the bottom of the problem.

Is a college education as important for a girl as it is for a boy?

Yes. A woman with a college educaction, particularly with an advanced degree, has a good chance of getting an excellent job.

Offhand, I can think of at least three good reasons for a girl's education being important. In the first place, she should have a chance in life to do what she wants, whether it's being a registered nurse, a professional photographer, or president of a bank. Secondly, in the event of marriage, the first several years can be pretty hard on young couples. A working wife bringing in a good salary, and enjoying herself at the same time, can benefit a marriage.

Finally, if a girl becomes a homemaker and mother, her husband will spend his time earning a living and constantly be exposed to new experiences. It's like the old story about the young mother of four who one day took a shopping trip by herself. While riding on a bus, she sighted a train in the distance. She automatically turned to the man at her left to say, "See the pretty choo-choo?" If a woman doesn't have enough education to keep her mind stimulated in the years of domestic captivity child bearing brings on, her husband may outgrow her, and the marriage will stagnate.

My daughter wants to go to college to find a husband. I feel the money could be better used for one of my other children who really wants an education. Should I go along with her or say no?

It seems a little shallow for a girl to regard a college as a hunting ground for eligible males. If a compromise can be worked out in which you help financially to the degree you are able, and your daughter gets a job to meet the rest of her expenses, I think that would be the best solution.

I certainly wouldn't deprive a promising younger child the benefit of college in order to provide the older daughter with social contacts.

We have been putting money into a college fund for our children. Now it's almost time for them to go, but the colleges seem to have become hotbeds of revolutionaries and dope addicts. What can we do?

Television and the newspapers have done a good job of making the colleges appear in constant turmoil and, in some few cases, they are right. The trouble is the schools without problems don't make the news. It is true that teenagers are going to be exposed to new ideas and values, no matter where they attend college; however, the manner in which they've been raised will determine how they'll react. And remember: Kids can use drugs or learn revolutionary ideas on the streets, as well as in college, but they can't get a degree on the streets.

We can't afford to send our children to a university. Do city junior colleges have much to offer?

Yes. City junior colleges have the benefit of being free, in most cases, to area residents. Many of these colleges also offer intensive specialized study in commercial fields: data processing; police, automotive, and secretarial sciences; television and radio broadcasting; photography; etc., which many larger universities don't offer.

Some four-year colleges and universities will only take credits from specific junior colleges. If your child intends to transfer to a four-year school, make sure beforehand that school will accept his or her credits. Also a couple of years at a junior college gives a student an opportunity to prove himself at little cost to the family. If the teenager's grades are outstanding, there will be a chance at a scholarship.

How are scholarships awarded?

Scholarships are generally granted on the basis of athletic and scholastic achievement in high school, and outstanding scores on state scholarship exams and national scholastic achievement tests, but in some cities, there are also service awards for outstanding service to the community. The admittance office at a college will provide a complete listing of the scholarships available at that particular school. Some colleges are noted for liberal scholarship programs.

My son made top grades in high school, and now he wants to get a job. My wife is pushing him toward college. I feel caught in the middle and don't know what line to take.

There are many factors to be considered. Does the boy have a scholarship which must be taken advantage of the following semester? Would the scholarship make it possible for him to attend a school he wouldn't be able to otherwise? If he goes to college immediately, is your income great enough to cover all his expenses, or will he have to take a part-time job while he is attending?

If he doesn't have a scholarship, I think it would be a good idea for him to take a job now and work for a year or two, before going back to school. This will help him get an accurate picture of what field he is interested in and what further education he needs to compete in that field. There are many ways in which to get an education. Night school and correspondence schools can be taken advantage of until a time when the boy will want to attend a college full-time.

After attending school for twelve years, a practical education in the working world is an advantage. Don't forget that the nice thing about good high school grades is that they don't change. They are like money in the bank and can be reinvested in college any time at all.

My husband wants our son to become a lawyer; the boy wants to be an artist. My husband always wanted to be a lawyer. What do you suggest?

I would suggest that your husband take a night course in beginning law. That may sound like a cold answer, but it would give your husband an outlet for his own frustrations and interests.

I have a great sympathy for young people who are interested in the fine arts. I would like to pass on a bit of advice to the boy, however. It's not easy. I've been writing for about eight years. I have a scrapbook full of rejection slips from some of the best publishers in this country, and my first published book fell flat on its binding. It took six years to get that book off the ground, and that's considered fast. I know writers, good writers, who have tried, without success, for fifteen years and longer to get a book published.

It's a long, up-hill fight, all the way. It takes

discipline and devotion. A person finds out fast whether or not he's cut out for it when the rejections come. All the people I know in the arts have pumped a lot of gas.

There is another point to be considered. Not all artists are starving. There are great futures in commercial art, drafting, and architectural design. A few years at an art school will give an artist an adequate background to launch him into both a fulfilling and profitable career.

Let the boy find out what his chances are. He could change his goals in a year, and decide that law school would provide him with a brighter future.

Is there any way to keep teenagers interested in school and aware of the benefits of education?

That depends on the teenagers and the parents. Some teenagers want to experience life firsthand, and feel that school is interfering with their education.

But you can try to stimulate your children intellectually by holding lively discussions on subjects of current interest and by making regular trips to the local library with them. If education and reading are valued in your home, no matter how much the children rebel, they will retain these values as they mature.

If you take an active interest in those subjects your teenagers are enthusiastic about, and bring to the children enthusiasms of your own, they can't help but grow and expand intellectually.

Of course, the benefits of an education can be pointed out simply by comparing the career possibilities of a person who has an education with a person who doesn't. Exploring vocations and careers together will also help your children realize their own potential.

Chapter 3

PETTING TO PREGNANCY:
HOW TO AVOID IT

We attend a lot of movies as a family. Our children, ages fourteen and seventeen, have asked to go to a couple of popular, but questionable, films. Should we include this type of entertainment in family viewing?

Personally, I'm against censorship in any form. I think parents should exercise their own judgment regarding what films the family should see. I'd suggest reading the movie reviews in the family magazines to get an idea of a picture's suitability for your teenagers. If you are still in doubt, go see the picture yourself, first.

While the best movies I've seen in the past six or seven years have underplayed sex, nudity, and offensive language, there are exceptions. *American Graffiti* included a lot of four-letter words, but it was in an effort to accurately depict the language of high school teenagers in the late 1950s, and overall it was a good film.

Our daughter is in her second year of junior high school and has already been asked for a date. Isn't this too young?

Not necessarily. Kids today often start dating in junior high, and, in some respects, it's perfectly healthy. Most kids go through a period of hating the opposite sex, and early dating can relax tensions somewhat between the sexes. There are many wholesome activities young teens can do together in groups or as couples, this way learning to respect and enjoy each other's company. In other words, kids can become friends with members of the opposite sex before sexuality and all its hard-hitting emotional implications become a major problem.

I think some types of dates are all right for my fourteen-year-old, but kids today seem far more advanced than when I went to school. Are they?

Yes! That is one of the problems with early dating. Today's teenagers are exposed to the facts of physical sex before they can possibly understand the emotional implications. It is up to the parents to bring the mysterious subject of sex out in the open. Teenagers may know something of the facts of life and have learned half-truths from friends and sexually exploitive entertainment. But it's your job to clear up any confusion, provide information, state your feelings, your values, and offer guidelines of behavior.

*My daughter is only fifteen, but she is well built
and looks older. One day when we were
downtown, three hoodlum types on motorcycles
whistled at her and yelled something about
"rape bait." I've been scared to death ever
since. I can't very well change her looks, but
I feel like I have to do something.*

Certain teenage boys will yell almost anything
at girls to attract attention to themselves. But
the threat of rape is a very serious concern.

Parents should warn their daughters to avoid
situations which can lead to rape: hitchhiking,
hanging around bars, or being picked up by
strange guys. Every girl should also learn some
basic self-defense strategies; she can do much to
dissuade an attacker with a simple action like
dragging her heel across his shin bone. Hat pins,
hair spray, plastic squeeze lemons (aimed at his
eyes), nail files, and lighted cigarettes are a few
of the self-defense weapons she can carry, if she
must be out alone late at night.

Your local police headquarters or National
Organization for Women (NOW) Center will
have information concerning self-defense classes;
the fees are usually nominal.

*The styles girls are wearing now are terrible.
How can I convince my daughter she's too
sexy for her own good?*

It's hard to convince anyone of anything. You
might contact the police to see if they would show
your daughter photographs of women who had
been molested. They won't be pretty pictures,
but maybe the shock value will have its effect on

your daughter. Clothes that suggest a girl is promiscuous can create risky situations, not only with outright strangers, but with dates, as well.

I've heard that some of the kids are sunbathing nude at a secluded beach, but I didn't think my daughter was one of them until I noticed she didn't have any tan lines from her bathing suit. Should I say anything about it?

Yeah. Preferably in private, if possible. There's nothing particularly wrong with sunbathing in the raw, if you have a nice private backyard to do it in, but nude beaches attract all kinds of kooks. Your daughter should be aware of the risk involved if she and her friends run into a nut. Not only that, if your daughter is going to the beach with both boys and girls, the girls are asking for trouble, no matter how nice, liberal, and sophisticated the boys are.

Our daughter was molested when she was seven. We thought she had adjusted, but now she seems to shy away from boys at an age when most of her friends are dating. What should we do?

Talk about it with her. There might be a lingering fear which you could help alleviate through a calm discussion. Normally, I'm against parents setting their children up with dates, but in this case your daughter may feel more comfortable inviting, or having you invite, the son of a friend or associate on a family outing. Discuss the possibilities with her and see how she feels.

If she's completely against even discussing the

issue, she might have a problem serious enough to warrant seeing a professional counselor or clergyman.

Our daughter hasn't had a single date even though she's nearly seventeen. She says she hasn't met any boys who interest her and when she does, she'll date. Until then, it's just a waste of time. Is this normal?

Your daughter sounds pretty mature. There are too many campus queens who are trying to win popularity contests and miss out on the joys of being a teenager. Give the girl time. Unless she's a total recluse and has no girl friends either, my bet is that she'll come out a stable, interesting and well-adjusted person.

Should we allow our sixteen-year-old daughter to go steady?

There's plenty of time to devote to one person after you get married; the teenage years should be a time for fun, a time for getting to know different people. Dating one person exclusively naturally limits one's experience.

Talk it over with your daughter. If she has a strong feeling for the boy, and they enjoy each other's company, leave them alone. When they stop having an agreeable relationship, they'll break it off. Many teenagers do go steady with several people before they get out of high school, and often to them going steady only means they are seeing more of one person than anyone else at the time.

Our daughter is only sixteen, and she's sure she's madly in love with this twenty-two-year-old creep. We can't stand him, and we're sure he's no good. How can we put a stop to it?

There are laws against relationships with minors in many states. Maybe you could have a restraining order invoked against him, maybe even hit him with a statutory rape beef.

The problem is your daughter probably *is* in love with the creep. Sometimes that's a more powerful love than comes in later years. It's for certain your daughter sees the guy in a different light than you do. To her, he must be a pretty nice guy. If he's as bad as you think, chances are he'll show that side of himself to her sooner or later, and all you can do is hope she won't get too torn up in the process. People seldom marry their first love. Keep your cool and wait it out.

Invite the boy to your house as often as possible and try to discover things to like about him. Maybe having people show an interest in him is all that he needs to stop being a creep. If not, it's a lot easier to take advantage of a girl with a set of phantom parents you've never met than it is to pull something with a girl whose folks you know. If that sounds like experience talking, I've been labeled a creep a couple of times myself.

Whatever you do, don't put him down. Having to defend him will make her pull away from you and push her closer toward him.

I'm stuck. My seventeen-year-old daughter has asked me to OK birth control pills for her. Should I?

That would depend on you. If you have no

serious moral objections to your daughter having a sexual relationship with someone she cares about, by all means help her protect both herself, the boy, and you. Since she has come to you for help, it's obvious that you have established a good rapport with her.

If you do have serious objections, explain them to her. Your daughter sounds like the kind of girl who wouldn't be against taking other viewpoints into consideration. Of course, you'll have to accept her decision. She has to establish her own set of values, and they may not always agree with yours. That is no reason to let them stand in the way of what is obviously a good relationship otherwise.

If your daughter does decide on birth control pills, it would probably make you feel better to have a session with a counselor or other adviser in conjunction with her medical exam.

My daughter is sixteen and has admitted to having had three love affairs in the past year. To me this is promiscuous, but she claims that times have changed, and there's nothing wrong with casually sleeping with someone you care for. What can I do?

It's time for a talk. Explain some of the facts. Casual sexual relationships will make her more vulnerable to both pregnancy and venereal disease. But more important, casual relationships do not offer the rewards of a deeper, emotional relationship. Everyone is looking for affection, love, sharing, and commitment. She's kidding herself if she thinks she'll find these things by jumping into bed with every guy who turns her on. Sex isn't an end in itself. If she thinks it is, she's been misled by some of her friends.

Chastity belts are out of style, and once you've warned her of the problems involved, keep the lines of communication open.

If it really offends you to have your daughter live this way at your expense, and she won't listen to reason, you might want to take some stronger steps. You can suggest that she'll either have to abide by your house rules, talk with a professional counselor, or become self-supporting.

Our daughter is sixteen and pregnant.
Where do we go from here?

The first step is to a doctor. Every moment of pregnancy is important and a doctor's care can't begin too soon. In the event that an abortion is desired, arrangements should be made early.

From this point on, life will be one continuing jumble of hassles and mixed emotions. Confrontations with the boy and his parents are inevitable, but try to remain mature and don't give in to hysterics. Everyone from brothers and sisters of the kids to the grandparents have to keep talking. Silence in a case like this does little or no good; it only compounds bad feelings. One more thing to remember, parents are there to help, not make decisions for other people's lives, even if the people involved are teenagers.

Our daughter didn't tell us she was pregnant
until it was too late for an abortion. Where do
we go for financial help in having this baby?

Taking for granted that the boy and his family

are unwilling or unable to help, try calling the local Federal Information Center. They will refer you to either a state agency or a private foundation able to help. Two of the options open to you are a home for unwed mothers, or a county adoption agency might offer information regarding adopting parents, who are willing to foot the medical bills.

Where can abortion information be obtained?

The best organization for problem pregnancy counseling that I've found is Planned Parenthood. They are a nationwide organization and offer a complete line of services. I might add that the staff at Planned Parenthood is composed of concerned individuals who believe in offering help without hassles. If a girl decides to have an abortion, Planned Parenthood will make hospital referrals.

My daughter is eighteen and has an illegitimate child. She's been lounging around the house for three months, and if she found a job, it would be good for all of us. The problem is that I can't take care of the baby. Where can we find out about day-care centers?

Right now your guess is as good as mine. The lack of day-care centers is a problem which has not been given the recognition it deserves. A central list of day-care centers is only in the planning stage. Two sources may provide a clue. They are the United Way office, which in some areas *might* be able to supply phone numbers of information and referral agencies, and the National Organization for Women (NOW), which is somewhat better equipped to help, but here again their information is limited. Checking the phone book for nursery schools and running them down one by one is about the only other course to follow.

My nineteen-year-old daughter recently told me she fears she's frigid. She says a boy can only arouse her to a certain point, then she gets cold. Does she need a psychiatrist?

It's possible. More probable is that she's just cautious about finding the right boy before chancing a mistake. I don't presume to understand the female mind, but even though this can be an emotional problem for a few more years, I'm inclined to think that once she finds a guy she's sure about, there won't be a problem. If her fear and coldness were to continue through a prolonged courtship with a guy she felt deeply toward, then outside help might be in order. I hope your daughter has sense enough to listen to her emotions for a while longer and not jump into anything through a fear of not being normal.

Is it all right for a seventeen-year-old girl to dress like a longshoreman?

I guess so. Dress styles for girls range from the ridiculous to the sublime. I'm not sure what the big attraction in dockworker styles is, but a lot of girls are dressing that way. A few years ago it was flowing robes and beads; in a few more, it could be fig leaves. Don't worry about it.

*Should parents allow their daughter to neck with
her boyfriend in the living room? We're
usually upstairs when this happens.*

I used to date a girl when I was in high school,
and we spent a lot of time on the back porch.
Her parents were in the kitchen. Every once in
awhile, her dad would come out to empty the
garbage and make some kind of joking remark,
like, "I'd better go back in, my glasses are getting
steamed up out here." We were happy; the folks
were happy; and nobody got pregnant.

Pregnancy can occur in back seats of cars, in
parks, on couches, or anywhere else it's convenient
and at any time of day, but it usually doesn't
occur in front of witnesses. Let the kids do their
thing, but develop a habit of getting drinks of
water downstairs—often.

*Our daughter seems to be leading a secret life.
She won't share any of her school or social
problems with us. She's a nice girl otherwise.
Her father and I have no idea about what's going
on. How can we get her to open up?*

The super-privacy thing is normal in teenagers.
It's usually just a phase, while they find out who
they are. Don't pressure her to tell you things,
but do show her that you are interested. If she
does tell you something, don't ask a lot of questions, just let her talk. Don't try to give her advice, unless she asks for it and then keep it brief.
She has to feel that she can confide in you without getting the third degree or being preached to,
before she will be willing to share her feelings
with you.

Don't let it throw you if, when she does open up, you hear things you didn't want to hear or that don't agree with your own beliefs. Let her be herself and recognize that with teenagers, their moods can change a dozen times a day and so can their ideas.

I'm having trouble getting my daughter to introduce her dates to us. How do you go about getting boys into the house?

I'd tell the girl I wanted to meet her dates simply out of a genuine interest in the fellows, not because I didn't trust her. Tell her that if she meets interesting people, of either sex, you'd like to meet them, too. Get the idea out of her head that you want to pry or stand in judgment of the boys. One more thing, when she does bring a boy home, follow through, and do show interest in him.

My fifteen-year-old daughter wants to go on an overnight trip with several other girls and boys. Should I allow it?

Only if a parent accompanies the group as a chaperone.

My son isn't going out with girls. He spends most of his time up in his room looking at "girlie" magazines. I know that masturbation is accepted as normal now, but I still don't think this is healthy. Is it?

It isn't unhealthy. Masturbation's only danger is in the exclusiveness of the act. If masturbation takes the place of normal heterosexual social contact after a certain age, then it becomes a problem. Living in a fantasy world isn't good for anybody. It tends to cut one off from reality.

My son is fifteen and he's running around with the biggest nineteen-year-old sissy I've even seen in my life. I want to talk to my boy about it, but how can I do it without a lot of embarrassment?

The best way to treat the subject is in the most straightforward manner possible. Ask your son's opinion about his friend's peculiarities. Don't approach the issue from the standpoint of your being afraid of the other boy's influence on your son. Act as though you are simply curious about him. No subject is embarrassing in itself. Embarrassment comes from one person feeling that the other person disapproves of him and is accusing him of something he should be ashamed of.

Should I allow my seventeen-year-old son to have his girl friend in his room with the door closed? They claim to be studying, but I'm not sure just what they are studying.

We've established that pregnancy can occur anywhere, any time. Having parents around is sometimes appreciated by teenagers. With partial privacy they can still neck but not go all the way. Sometimes complete privacy can pressure them into going too far, simply because they feel they shouldn't waste an opportunity. Just let them know you're around, and knock before going into the room. Besides, they might really be studying.

My daughter is dating a boy who drives what my husband calls a "four-wheel motel." It is a van, painted in wild colors with curtains and a mattress in back. There is even a bumper sign that reads, "Don't laugh—your daughter could be in back!" Should we continue to let her date him?

As long as he is a nice guy, I think it's OK. Most of those vans are for show. The fact that there is a mattress around doesn't mean it is being used. Floors, parks, and front seats serve the same purpose; a mattress only provides a little comfort. If the kids want to neck, they're going to find a place to accomplish it, anyway.

Our son is nearly nineteen and has been dating a fourteen-year-old girl. I'm afraid he's headed for trouble. What should I do?

Talk to people. For a short list, include your son, the girl, her parents, and a lawyer. The biggest hassle in a situation like this is when nobody knows what anyone else is feeling. It's possible that your son could be faced with charges for just going out with the girl. If you and her parents have an understanding, chances are they'll come to you rather than call the police in the event they get upset.

My son is fifteen. He's been seeing a much older girl who works as a waitress at a local hangout. Should I be concerned?

Concerned? Sure! What parent wouldn't be? If there's a man in the family, this is a job for him.

Your son should know about life, not the birds and the bees facts, but the older woman part of life. I'm sure that he's learning quite a bit from the girl, but he should have an adult male talk with him.

Many young boys go through a stage in which they have a great need to talk with an older girl. It's not unusual for a woman to have the same need for a younger boy. Some fine relationships develop this way. Don't push your son, but try to get him to bring the girl home for dinner some night or include her in a family outing.

The boy's emotional attachment to the girl could be a potential problem. In most male-female relationships, the guy gets more hung up in the beginning. Chances are, when it ends, the boy is going to get hurt. There's not too much you can do about that; when the time comes, just leave him alone and let him get over it.

I found a condom in my son's wallet. Should I say anything about it?

Not unless you're willing to explain to him what you were doing in his wallet in the first place. Either he's using a condom to avoid getting a girl pregnant or he's following the peculiar custom among teenage boys of carrying one to impress his friends. Drop the matter.

Our boy is sixteen and has been dating a girl a year younger. Her parents caught them petting, and now they are bringing statutory rape charges against our son. How can we fight it?

Get yourself a lawyer immediately! Then try to *peaceably* contact the girl's parents. If they are not agreeable to talking with you about it, drop it. Let the courts and lawyers handle it.

Our son is not quite seventeen and has gotten his sixteen-year-old girl friend pregnant. The kids say they want to get married, and her parents have agreed to sign. We think the marriage would be a mistake for our boy and could ruin his chances at a career. Should we sign anyway?

Teenage marriages have a high mortality rate. This doesn't mean that your son has no chance of having a good marriage, only that his chances would be better with fewer complications. A teenage marriage can also limit his opportunities for success; responsibilities do have a way of overriding things like college.

If the kids want to accept the responsibilities of their situation, it sounds like they are the kind of people with the personal integrity to work out other problems in life. If they are unrealistic in their approach to what's happening, you should try to make them aware of the problems they will face.

But you must remember that they are individuals with real emotions. Sometimes it's necessary to let them make their own mistakes, no matter how many misgivings you may have. They deserve a chance and all the help you can give them.

My son and his girl friend are both eighteen. Last week her parents came home early and caught them making love. They didn't even let her pack before throwing them out of the

house. My husband and I are very fond of the
girl and were only too happy to have her move
in here. The kids have been sleeping together
for two years, have been very careful about
birth control, and plan to be married as soon
as my son finishes his first two years of college.
They are both helpful, honest kids, and we don't
have any objections to the relationship. The
problem is that they have asked our permission
to share the same room. She has been sleeping in
the guest room up until now, and we can't decide
whether to go along with them or insist on a
wedding now. What do you think?

There is nothing unique about what happened.
Many teens and parents find themselves in the
same situation. Not many people handle it as well
as you seem to have.

As far as the immediate problem is concerned,
the answer depends upon your personal values.
The fact that the kids came to you with their
request indicates they have respect and apprecia-
tion for both you and the sanctity of your home.
If you object to their sharing the same room, I'm
sure they will understand your position.

You didn't state whether or not there were
other children in the house, but their presence
also would have to be taken into consideration.
The effect on younger brothers or sisters is very
important, and if the arrangement is agreed upon,
it must be made certain that the younger children
understand the special nature of the circumstances.

The probable reason for the kids not wanting
to get married now is finances. If getting married
wouldn't place them in a difficult financial posi-

tion, and you can continue to support them while your son goes to college, then there should be no objection to marriage. Or is there a problem in their relationship, which they want to work out before marriage? The kids may feel that they have a right to test a complete relationship before making it permanent. It appears they both recognize your right not to approve of such an arrangement and their right to carry one on.

Under the circumstances and considering the apparent maturity of the people involved, it is necessary for the four of you to discuss it in the most intimate manner. If, after discussing all the pros and cons, neither marriage nor the sharing of a room is feasible, you can still be of great help to the kids. Try to arrange times when they can have the house to themselves, or mutually agree that there will be nights when they don't come home.

The one thing to try to achieve is complete honesty amongst the four of you.

This may not seem like much of a problem, but my son is a streaker. What should I do about it?

Streaking is a fad, much like swallowing goldfish was in the forties or hanging a bare rear end (a "BA") out of a car window was in the fifties. Grin and bare it.

I've been divorced for ten years. The man I remarried two years ago is wonderful, both to me and the kids. The problem is my daughter is seventeen and runs around the house in little or nothing. I don't think there is anything to worry about, but I don't like the way my new

*husband sometimes looks at her. Should
I say anything?*

Not to your husband. Tell your daughter, no
matter how much she loves and trusts her step-
father, he's still a man, and she should respect
that fact by wearing clothes around him. Why
invite trouble?

*I want my teenagers to be aware of the problems
they may encounter with venereal disease.
Where do I find information on the subject?*

Many schools now have health education classes
which include a discussion of venereal diseases
as a part of the course. Unfortunately, the schools
often don't introduce the subject early enough,
and, in many cases, it comes too late to be of any
value. You could check with your school to see
how much information is available, and at what
grade level it is introduced.

Any doctor can also give you the information
you need, especially those doctors connected with
city or county clinics, or write to the Department
of Health, Education and Welfare in Washington
and request literature on the subject. Public libraries also have VD information available.

The best way to present the subject is in a
straightforward manner. It's your job to make
sure your teenagers recognize the symptoms of
the disease and know where they can go for help.

*I've discussed VD with my kids and told them
never to hesitate to come to me with this
problem, although I'm not sure that they would
want to confide in me. Is there a way for a*

teenager to get help without parents becoming involved?

Yes. Most doctors will treat teenagers without asking questions, and the public health services in many cities provide free medical treatment for venereal diseases. The person with VD is asked to provide the public health investigators with the names of all persons with whom there has been sexual activity, but these names are kept confidential. Parents are not notified of a teenager's visit.

Chapter 4

RELIEF IS JUST A SWALLOW AWAY

What is the difference between casual drug usage and addiction?

It can be compared to the difference between social drinking and alcoholism. Many of today's young, and not so young, people use sedatives, marijuana, stimulants, and even hallucinogens socially, the same way other people drink cocktails. The real problem with drugs is their extreme addictive potential, both physically and psychologically. And most persons will disregard the possibility of their own addiction in the firm belief that it can't happen to them.

I think my teenager has been smoking marijuana. Is there a way to be sure?

I can give you the symptoms of marijuana

usage, but with many people it is extremely difficult to tell because the physical symptoms are slight. Sometimes there is a dilation of the pupils, but not always. Sometimes there is a difficulty in coordinating, but, again, not always.

The most obvious symptoms are behavioral. A person stoned on grass may be slightly disoriented. He or she might not be aware of how much time has passed and become overly involved in an activity, spending an unsual amount of time completely absorbed in a television program, book, or music. After a few hours of being stoned the person often becomes ravenously hungry, especially for sweets. Another symptom is apathy. A normally energetic person may want to do nothing but sit and stare into space for hours at a time.

Marijuana can be dark green, light green, yellowish, or light brown in color and resembles the herb oregano to a degree. It is often stored in a plastic bag, and there may be short, light brown or light green stems and seeds in the package. The seeds are hard, shiny, and look like miniature cantaloupes with a small point on one end.

Grass is sold by the "lid" or "can," at least that's what we used to call it. Dope terminology changes about once a year. A lid is about one ounce, or an amount two or three fingers high, packed loose in the bottom of a sandwich-size plastic bag.

Grass often has a heavy odor, both before and after being smoked. The smell of marijuana smoke has been described as being sickeningly sweet or acrid, like burning hemp, neither of which accurately describes it. It has a unique smell, which can be detected from a great distance.

It is so difficult to tell if a person has been smoking marijuana by his behavior alone that many police departments now show their rookies grass and burn it for them so they will be able to recognize it in the future. You can also call or visit your local law enforcement agency to find out if they have a drug program to help parents recognize symptoms of drug usage.

My kids are curious about what being high on pot is like. Is there a way to describe it without actually experiencing it?

Not really. It's kind of like having a head stuffed with cotton candy. You have no sense of time and you can become completely absorbed in anything. Reality ceases to exist; fantasy becomes reality. It's kind of like being drunk without being dizzy or sick. It could be compared to the feeling a person who has never smoked gets when he inhales his first cigarette, only magnified about a thousand times.

Supposedly, the first experience with marijuana doesn't produce any noticeable reaction, but the first time I tried it, my legs felt like they were made out of rubber, and I felt like I was walking on the moon. I didn't realize I was stoned until I noticed six corpulent members of the Los Angeles Police Department at a traffic accident and laughed myself silly at the sight of them for no good reason. That's about the best I can do.

What is hash?

Hashish is the condensed resin of the female

hemp plant. It looks like brown tar and is usually about the size of a half stick of gum, chewed, which is the average amount, approximately a gram, purchased at a time.

Hash is usually smoked in a pipe, and a very minute amount produces a stronger effect than grass does, and a slightly different high. It's a difficult concept to understand, but hash makes your head feel tighter, as though it were bound with steel. It's also difficult to understand why that sensation would be pleasurable, but some people like it.

Are the kids smoking opium? I've heard rumors, but I always think of opium as being something out of the Tong wars.

The kids are smoking, at one time or another, everything they can get their hands on. Back in the sixties, it was banana peels, and I knew some people who went so far as to smoke coconut husks. Coconut husks don't do anything but tear your throat to pieces.

Opium isn't as widely used as marijuana and hash because of its cost and the difficulty in obtaining it. In 1969, the wholesale price was $450 for four ounces. And street prices can be triple or quadruple the wholesale price.

The effects of opium are also different than those of other smokables. When a person smokes opium, the usual procedure is to nod off into a drugged slumber filled with magnificent dreams and hallucinations. It's not a high like that of grass or hash, and some consider it the trip to beat all trips.

My sixteen-year-old has admitted smoking grass and hash, and I need some valid arguments against it. In what ways are these drugs dangerous?

Perhaps the main danger in getting high from these drugs is that they dull your senses. A lot of people claim that they heighten senses, especially taste buds and sexual sensations. To a certain extent, this is true. However, while one sense is sharpened through concentration on a single object, for example, the petals of a flower, the other senses that keep a person from doing things like walking in front of a bus are completely wiped out.

Another major hassle with using these drugs is that they make a person, after prolonged use, lazy and completely lacking in incentive. A lot of people I know claim this is not true, but I've watched people, who have smoked grass for ten years, and there is no denying the negative effects.

It is my hope that young people will listen to a man who is not a doctor or researcher, but who speaks from his own experience. In the sixties, I was an addict, a pusher, a thief, and a street hood. I was there, I know what I'm talking about. I'm grateful I stopped using drugs when I did, and I hope the experience, which almost ruined my life, can help keep other kids from having to go through the same pain and misery.

I overheard my seventeen-year-old say he had the "munchies." Isn't this a drug term?

It started out as a drug term. The miserable marijuana munchies described the hunger pangs associated with the use of marijuana. Later on, the term munchies was used by anyone who wanted a snack.

It may sound silly, but if I allow my kids to smoke cigarettes now, won't it be easier for them to graduate to grass later on?

Not necessarily. I know a lot of people who use grass, but won't touch tobacco. It's hard to dissuade kids from smoking; the best example is the one the parents themselves set. It's a funny thing about smoking. I kicked a habit that ran up to a hundred pills a day by stopping cold in one day, but after nine years, I can't seem to shake cigarettes.

My teenager has decided to be honest with me and has admitted using grass. He now wants to be allowed to smoke grass at home. His reasoning is it is better to use grass in the home where you are less likely to get hurt or arrested. Should I let him?

He's right about home being the safest place to use grass, but it is still against the law to possess marijuana. If you allowed him to use grass in your home, in many areas of the country you would be committing a felony. Don't complicate the issue by being a party to it. Inform your teenager that no matter what your views or his views are on grass, the police and courts take a different position.

Why let a lightweight matter like grass disrupt your whole family?

Since so many people agree that grass is not harmful, shouldn't it be legalized?

In the first place, I don't agree with all these "expert opinions" on the harmless nature of grass. From personal knowledge, no amount of research is *ever* going to convince me it is harmless. On the other hand, it is possible to get sentenced to twenty or more years in prison in some states for simple possession. That, too, is wrong.

I would like to see the penalties for possession of grass reduced. I think a system of progressive fines should be imposed for possession, possibly linked with a mandatory examination by a psychiatrist, in order to help people with "addictive personalities."

Stiffer fines and progressive jail sentences should be reserved for the pusher. I'd suggest a minimum of 180 days for the first offense, one year for the second, two years for the third, four for the fourth, eight for the fifth, and ten years for each conviction after the fifth. Perhaps the pusher will think twice about going back into business if he knows he will have a stiffer sentence to serve if caught again.

Is it true that the use of grass leads to harder drugs?

That question brings to mind the familiar line, not all grass users go on to heroin, but all heroin users started on grass. Smoking grass doesn't cause a craving for harder drugs; however, often it puts a person in contact with other people using and selling harder drugs. It's the ready availability of these drugs and perhaps the desire to experiment that causes a teenager to move on to the harder stuff.

Our two teenagers, sixteen and seventeen, are against the use of drugs, but they both want to be allowed to use alcohol at home, as well as at parties. Should we go along with this?

As parents, you should examine your own drinking habits and your feelings about alcohol—its use and abuse. I can't prescribe or prohibit its use for teenagers.

The fact that there are nine million alcoholics in this country and an estimate of another twenty million with a drinking problem proves that alcohol is not to be taken lightly. And there have been recent television programs documenting the growing problem of teenage alcoholism.

If you do decide to give the kids a green light, approach the subject of alcohol by explaining how you feel about its use, what happens when somebody drinks to excess and how, like drugs, it can be used as an escape to avoid problems and ultimately become a deadly crutch.

As far as drinking at teenage parties goes, caution the kids to control their intake. Kids will often be tempted to gulp drinks at a party to obtain instant relaxation; they're drunk before they know what hit them. If they've had more than one drink, they shouldn't drive.

There is not much more you can do except prohibit it entirely if you are strongly against their drinking.

We had it out last year over the pot business. Our teen promised to quit using it and has.

*Now a plastic bag with four red capsules in it
has popped up. How can I find out what they are?*

The most obvious way might not be the best,
under the circumstances, but you could ask the
kid. If you "had it out" on the subject of grass,
it sounds as though communication may be a
problem in your household. That's not to say that
arguments or anger are not good; anger should
be expressed, but you have to talk as well as yell.

If you can't ask your kid what the pills are,
try your family druggist or doctor. The public library should have a pharmacist's encyclopedia
with descriptions and pictures of drugs. The
police can also help in identifying drugs, but you
can be sure that after they have answered your
questions, they will have a few of their own.

*I found a note from one of my fifteen-year-old's
friends asking about "scoring Rd's."
What does this mean?*

"Scoring" means procuring or obtaining something. "Rd's" are Red Devils, Reds, Fender-
Benders, War Pills, or Gorilla Pills. The technical
name is Seconal. Seconal comes in red gelatin
capsules and is a barbiturate used primarily as a
sleeping pill and, to a lesser extent, for pain.

What are the symptoms of barbiturate usage?

A person under the influence of barbiturates
has many of the same reactions as a drunk. That's
where the term "Fender-Benders" comes from.
Speech is slurred, and the one overriding symptom is sometimes described as "copping a Seconal

attitude." A person with a Seconal attitude is extremely beligerent. Most of the time, all they want to do is fight. They often become completely unreasonable and will viciously turn on friend and enemy alike.

My teenager came home one night acting drunk and later admitted to taking "downers." The only downers I had heard of were Reds, but the kid said he had taken "Rainbows," which aren't supposed to be as dangerous. Is this true?

No. Rainbows, which are Tuinals, are every bit as dangerous as any of the other downers. The most common downers are Seconals, Tuinals, and Nembutals, which come in yellow capsules and are known as Yellow Jackets or Abbots. Other sedatives and tranquilizers are also used by many teens, but they are not as dangerous as these three. Morphine and codeine are available, but because of their scarcity and high price, they aren't in common use.

What are M&M's?

"M&M's" are a peculiar concoction of Methedrine and morphine. This combination has also been called a "speed-ball," and heroin often is substituted for the morphine. It is one of the most volatile combinations, the one drug speeding up the system and the second fighting equally hard to slow it down.

The practice of mixing drugs is common. Marijuana, amphetamines, and beer are another favorite combination. Often an LSD trip will be tailed off by taking reds. These combinations are both potent and dangerous.

Our seventeen-year-old has been going through a lot of emotional turmoil with her boyfriend.
A friend gave her some Valium to help calm her down. Isn't this dangerous?

It's always dangerous to take someone else's medicine. Valium is a tranquilizer often prescribed by doctors for the kind of nervous problems your daughter has.

You should send your daughter to a doctor. If he feels she needs a tranquilizer or mood stabilizer, he'll prescribe it. She should be reminded, if she does get a prescription, that mixing Valium and alcohol can be lethal.

Our fifteen-year-old was badly frightened during an earthquake. Our doctor suggested Librium, but I'm afraid that establishing a pattern of relying on drugs could be harmful. Is this true?

You'll have to make your own decision as to whether or not to listen to your doctor. Doctors are becoming concerned about the practice of "pill-pushing." They are not in business to create drug users.

The drug your doctor suggested is mild and suited for the purpose you describe. It may be beneficial to your child.

My daughter wanted to lose weight and started taking diet pills. She lost the weight, hardly eats at all now, seems high all the time, and is still taking the pills. Is she hooked?

She could very well be. If she got the pills from a doctor, tell him about it, and see to it she doesn't get any more pills and does get counseling. If she got them from another source, take her to the doctor and tell him what the problem is. At any rate, get her to a doctor immediately.

I had suspected that my fourteen-year-old had been trying drugs, but until recently I had no proof. While putting away some clothes, I found a box with a hypodermic needle in the drawer. This is more serious than I realized. What is the best way to confront the child?

It may not work for everyone, but we had a similar situation in our family. My wife and I were at her parent's house one night, and my father-in-law, Eric, found a needle in my four-teen-year-old brother-in-law's dresser drawer. Greg wasn't at home at the time his dad found the needle, so Eric spent the next couple of hours discussing drugs with us.

Later, when Greg got home, Eric calmly put the needle on the table in front of him without saying a word. There was a moment of tense silence during which I lit a cigarette. Greg smoked, supposedly without his father's knowledge, and Eric was against smoking, having quit almost twenty-five years before. Suddenly Eric reached out, took my cigarette, inhaled deeply, and passed it to Greg. The suddenness of the act broke the tension, and we sat up discussing it until two in the morning.

As it turned out, the boy had stolen the needle

from the doctor's office on an impulse and wasn't quite sure how it was used. He had originally thought about selling it, but instead his father wound up using the needle to inject glue behind dry spots of wallpaper.

While this approach may not work for everyone, the element of surprise really does loosen up a conversation. Another approach might be for the mother to make a statement such as, "You know, I'm getting sick and tired of the garbage that passes for conversation in this house." Even if she doesn't get the results she wants, she will undoubtedly have the kid's full attention.

My teens are always saying, "Wow, what a rush!" Does this have anything to do with drugs?

It could. A rush is the term to describe the immediate sensation which comes from injecting drugs directly into the veins. Drugs taken orally can take anywhere from twenty minutes to an hour to take effect. Injected drugs hit within seconds. The sensation is much the same as that felt when the dentist gives a sodium pentothal injection in order to pull a tooth. The term is also used by teenagers to describe any normal feeling of exhilaration.

What does the term "maintain" mean?

To maintain is to act normally when under the influence of drugs or alcohol. A driver with one too many drinks under his belt would try to maintain when pulled over by a policeman.

We've heard a lot about "speed." What is it?

Originally speed was a nickname given to crystal Methedrine. Older drug users may refer to crystal Methedrine as "crystal," "meth," or "crank." Later, speed came into use to describe any stimulant, including Benzedrine, Dexedrine, Dexamyl, and all other amphetamines. Speed describes any drug that kills the appetite and steps up the nervous system.

How is speed taken?

Usually orally in the form of pills or tablets. In the case of crystal Methedrine, which comes in a powder, it can be taken orally or diluted in water and injected or inhaled, which is called sniffing or snorting.

What are the symptoms of using stimulants?

The physical symptoms of using stimulants are fairly noticeable, the most obvious is the person's agitation; he or she is extremely nervous. The pupils become dilated, and the person may be inclined to talk a lot, especially about philosophy, religion, and politics. A person using stimulants may also become very involved in strange activities, such as picking thousands of lint specks off of a sweater or counting blades of grass.

They say that speed kills. Does it?

Yeah. Speed kills in a number of ways. It is a very dangerous drug which can paralyze the respiratory system during an overdose or impair the body's ability to fight off disease. Some people become highly irrational under the influence of stimulants. Paranoia, a common symptom, can cause a person to attack a policeman, an innocent bystander, even a freight train.

Apparently a lot of kids are using "Bennys" to study. Do they really help?

To a certain extent they do. For one thing, they keep you awake while you are studying. For another, they increase your attention span. In the long run, taking amphetamines to study can help, but the overall effect on the memory isn't as beneficial as studying on your own, without stimulants.

A couple of my teenager's friends claimed that LSD brought about some sort of supernatural experience—a closeness to God and nature. Is this true?

In the mind of the person who has used LSD it probably did. LSD is such a strange drug that nobody is really sure what kind of reaction will occur or why. LSD, it is agreed, does produce visual hallucinations. It also produces mental hallucinations, which is the part of the mirage that speaks to you. Some people refuse to believe the visions they see and feel while under the influence of LSD are just the effects of the drug, and claim they have had a spiritual revelation.

Is LSD really as dangerous as they say it is?

LSD is like nitroglycerin. There is no way of predicting how it will affect the user. There is just no way of telling whether or not someone will be able to handle monsters chasing him, people changing color, or a hamburger suddenly coming to life and begging not to be eaten.

Anything can set a person taking LSD on an irreversible path toward insanity. Some people, in addition to experiencing hallucinations, may also deeply probe their own personalities. If they have traits they wish were different, they might spend hours berating themselves and finally, after deciding they don't deserve to live, attempt suicide. The "bummer" or "bad trip" can occur the first time LSD is used, the fiftieth time, or not at all. Years after an LSD trip a person can suddenly plunge into a hell of hallucinations he has no way of overcoming. As far as acid's effect on a person's chromosomes, research hasn't yet found the answer. There is no way to be certain it doesn't cause birth defects, either immediately or in future generations.

Our teenager has admitted using LSD. Should we have a doctor examine him?

It might not be a bad idea, but there probably won't be much the doctor can tell you. LSD doesn't show up on blood tests, nor can its future effects be predicted. In the event the teenager starts to behave strangely, then a doctor should certainly be contacted immediately.

Our daughter has tried LSD, and I'm worried. Isn't it more dangerous for a girl to use LSD than a boy?

Like I said, there just hasn't been enough research. Children are the product of two parents. They receive chromosomes from both. If female chromosomes can be damaged by LSD, the same would hold true for the male.

My wife and I used LSD before we were married, and, fortunately, our children are normal. If I had it to do over again, I wouldn't take the chance with my children's lives, and the thought that my grandchildren may suffer from my mistakes scares me to death.

Our daughter is sixteen and has tried grass and pills. What worries me is that drugs remove a person's inhibitions. Should I refuse to let her date unless she promises to quit?

There is a lot of street talk about which drug and how much will get a girl in bed, but I don't really know how much fact there is in it.

As far as getting your daughter to make promises not to take drugs because you fear she'll fall in bed with someone, you're attacking the problem from the wrong angle. Liquor also breaks down inhibitions, and if you knew your daughter sipped a cocktail now and then, would you make her quit dating? It would be wiser to discuss the effects of drugs and have a talk with her about men. Be concerned, not inquisitive. There's a difference. Show her you really care.

I was worried about my teenager sniffing glue, but he said he didn't because it put "cobwebs" in your brain. What are cobwebs?

The fumes from glue, gasoline, or other combustibles cause deterioration of the brain cells. Cobwebs is the term used to describe this deterioration. You're lucky that your son has picked up on this piece of street lore and taken it to heart. He's lucky too.

What are the symptoms of sniffing glue or other fumes?

Persons under the influence of glue or other fumes react in much the same manner as persons using barbiturates. They stagger and stumble, speech is slurred, and they become disoriented. Often they are antagonistic and beligerent.

The most obvious way of detecting a glue sniffer is by the heavy glue odor, both on the person's breath and in his clothes. Glue can be sniffed in two ways. If it's contained in a bag, a person can put his nose or mouth in the bag and inhale. Or sometimes the glue is put in a sock or rag; the rag or sock is put in the mouth, and the glue is inhaled orally.

Should I punish my child for using drugs, and if I should, how?

Once parents find out that their kids are using drugs, the biggest problem is in deciding what they should do about it. Drug usage doesn't fall into the same category as other misbehavior. Drug usage occurs because of a combination of emotions and circumstances unique to each person. A normal, healthy, socially active teenager can fall victim to drugs as easily as an underprivileged member of a minority group. Drugs show no respect for money or class.

The function of drugs also varies from person to person. Some users view drugs as a mystical step toward salvation, others use them as a trip into a sensual Disneyland, and still others, as an escape from economical or emotional problems.

Drug addiction is a hideous demon which operates with all the psychological stealth of a Protestant devil. This description may sound melodramatic, but if I had to find a perfect way of tricking people, I'd do it with drugs.

Chances are that kids using drugs, or for that matter anyone, will not recognize what's happening to them. The changes that take place in the personality are so gradual they go unnoticed.

Most teenagers don't see anything wrong with taking drugs. If parents punish kids for something the kids believe in or at the least don't see anything wrong with, the punishment seems ill-deserved. And, secondly, most teenagers think they are too old for punishment. The teenage years are just as difficult for teens as they are for parents. Punishment is not the answer.

What should parents do if they find out their teens are taking drugs?

That is a hard question to answer. At a luncheon for the San Fernando Valley Commission on Drug Abuse, not too long ago, a mother asked the same thing.

I suggested keeping the lines of communication open, maintaining your integrity without giving in to the impulse to preach, and loving the kid one hell of a lot. In other words, keep talking.

The time to get good family communication

started is long before the problem of drugs comes up, but it's never too late. Often, parents are surprised at their kid's involvement with drugs. Sometimes they take it as a personal reflection on their abilities as parents. However, drug users are found in the most open and loving families. In such families discussing the problem will not be difficult. Less fortunate families have twice the work ahead of them.

As far as maintaining integrity goes, set a good example for the kids. Kids are aware of their parents' faults, and the "Do as I say, not as I do" approach doesn't earn their respect. The manner in which parents handle their problems and spend leisure time will be thrown up to them if there is the slightest amount of hypocrisy in the advice they hand out.

If parents sympathetically share their own experiences, their mistakes, and point out what they have learned by them, the kids may not agree, but at least they won't reject their parents' counsel out of hand. Avoid a superior, disapproving air, and, above all, love the kids. And that's something parents are going to have to learn for themselves.

Chapter 5

STRUNG OUT!

What does the term strung out mean?

Strung out means dependent upon. The term can also imply heavy involvement with something. If a person is strung out on drugs, he could be taking them regularly, without being addicted.

Some people are heavy drug users, but aren't addicted. There are people, few in number, who have been using drugs heavily for many years. They learn to control their usage and to function somewhat normally in society.

If a person is using drugs every day, how can they not be addicted? I don't understand.

I think we're getting hung up in semantics. There is a definite dependency, but it may not be physical with these people. In other words, their bodies may not crave the drugs, but their minds must have them. Some people don't acknowledge this mental dependency as addiction, others do, but call it a psychological dependency. No matter how you want to categorize this type of drug usage, it all adds up to the same thing—strung out.

Are all heroin users addicts?

Not physically. There are heroin users who only take the drug occasionally, on weekends. They may not even use a needle. Heroin can be swallowed or inhaled, although it is generally injected with a needle.

"Joy- or skin-popping" describes the trip of the heroin user who injects it into his skin, instead of his veins. The high is about the same, but without the rush. These users don't have a physical craving for the drug, but a psychological dependency may develop. Many heroin addicts started out in this manner. It's a dangerous game to play.

What are the symptoms of heroin use?

Depending on how much of the drug has been taken and how often, the symptoms of heroin use may resemble those of barbiturates. The heroin user may appear intoxicated, but usually will not be violent or beligerent. A person using heroin will sit and nod, as though in some sort of dreamlike trance. A confirmed user will sniffle and scratch as the effects of the drug wear off, and the addict will show signs of nausea, vomiting, and possibly cramps.

In the movies, the police always taste the white powder and immediately know it's heroin. How is this test made?

Heroin used to be cut with quinine, and that was the substance they were looking for. Heroin itself has no taste or odor. Now it is cut with milk-sugar or even talc. Actual confirmation must be made in a lab.

What should a parent do if he discovers his teenager has been using heroin?

Get the kid to a doctor and fast. Second stop may be a psychiatrist. The teenager using heroin is in for a lot of trouble. He has to recognize the seriousness of his problem before he can be helped. This is a job for pros, and the teenager may not understand your turning him over to them, but it has to be done.

Our teenager has been using heroin and is now undergoing treatment. I've heard there's "no such thing as an ex-junkie." Is this true?

To a certain extent. Unfortunately, most of what the general public knows about drugs and addiction is learned from such "well-informed" sources as the *Adam-12* and *Marcus Welby* television programs and *The French Connection*.

Heroin can be cleaned out of the bloodstream, but eliminating the psychological dependency is another matter. There are users who leave the drug treatment centers and go directly to a connection to obtain more smack (heroin). Their personal problems and guilts, which make addiction a necessary way of life, haven't changed. They go back to the same environment with the same set of problems and the same way of coping —heroin.

Getting his head together is the hardest thing for the addict. A heroin addict has no hope. He feels his dreams have very little chance of fulfillment. Many teenage addicts are too young to recognize that things can change for them and too old not to notice the need for change. They can't decide where they're going, nor even where they want to go. A teenager feels like everyone else in the world has his life well ordered, except him. He feels different and isolated.

Sex is another large part of the problem. Teenagers are filled with conflicting emotions and physical desires. They feel the need for love and a physical, romantic relationship, and don't have the emotional ability to handle it. Drugs provide the answer. A teenager using drugs, especially heroin, doesn't have any problems. Heroin eliminates all conflict, initiative, and desire.

If a teenager can learn a new way to cope with these emotions and problems, without using drugs, perhaps through professional counseling, if he can begin to hope, find new dreams, and set realistic goals, then there's every chance for him to make it.

What is Synanon?

Synanon, founded by Charles Dederich, is a

live-in treatment center for the rehabilitation of addicts. It started out as the addicts' alternative to Alcoholics Anonymous.

At Synanon, the first step is overcoming the physical craving for drugs. During the physical withdrawal, the addict is given a lot of emotional support.

The next step, which takes time and effort, is to restructure the addict's personality—no small task. If the addict is willing to try to change, the Synanon members will attempt to help. It is accomplished through group discussions which force the addict both to see him or herself as he or she actually is and to reveal this self to others. The idea is to provide the addict with a basis for developing honest personal relationships. The participants, who are ex-addicts and nonaddicts, are encouraged to say what they feel, to be honest, even to the point of hostile confrontation.

Synanon has been compared to a Marine bootcamp. It is a closely regulated, structured society. There are definite rules, and those who break the rules are punished. The system of severe regulations is aimed at helping the addict cope with the rigorous demands of the larger world outside Synanon's walls.

Parents have been critical of Synanon because of its rule that the addict is not allowed to contact family or friends for an indefinite period of time after admission. Synanon feels that if the friends and family could have helped in the first place, there would be no need for the addict to have sought Synanon's aid. If you're not part of the answer, you must be part of the problem.

After he or she gets clean, the ex-addict has a

choice of leaving the community or remaining and becoming even more deeply involved in the Synanon life-style. The success rate at Synanon is so great, the courts will release addicts into Synanon's custody, instead of locking them up.

Are barbiturates addictive?

Yes. Barbiturates build up the same kind of dependencies heroin does.

I recently found out both my kids are heavily into barbiturates. I have decided to lock them in the house until I'm sure they're off the drugs. I've heard there is a withdrawal period. How long will it last, and is there anything I can do to make it easier on them?

Don't lock them in the house. They wouldn't understand. They'll resent your efforts, and probably go right back to drugs the minute they get free. A better alternative would be to make yourself available to them for help in kicking the habit. Remember: It is *their* habit.

If they do ask for help, you'll discover that drug withdrawal doesn't happen the way you see it depicted on television. The withdrawal period could last anywhere from two hours to two days, depending on how much of a hold the drugs have on their systems. The biggest hassle in withdrawal is the sickness and depression that comes with it from having a wornout system. This stage is like having a bad case of the flu and can last several weeks before real improvement is seen.

A friend of our seventeen-year-old's had an overdose at our house. Not knowing what to do, we called an ambulance. For future reference, what could we have done to treat him?

You did the best thing possible. Someone having an overdose (OD) needs hospital care, and they need it as soon as possible. The hospital will pump the victim's stomach (this must be done within two hours of taking the pills in order to do any good) and administer stimulants to counter the effect of the barbiturates or heroin.

If there is some reason the person can't be taken to a hospital immediately, there are some first aid measures you can apply, which are recommended by doctors. First, don't let the person sleep. If you have any stimulants such as diet pills, give the person one or two; if not, coffee will suffice—strong and black. Bread, cookies, popcorn, or any similar absorbent food should be given to the person. But make sure he doesn't choke.

Keep him active. Walk him in circles. Make him count your fingers. Have him repeat the alphabet. Put cold water on the face and chest; it will shock his system, and adrenalin is one thing that will counteract downers. If no more than two hours have passed since the person took the drugs, try to get him to vomit by making him drink hot water and mustard, but, again, be careful not to choke him. This procedure takes about three hours, and the person giving the help should be prepared for an exhausting and frightening job. *It's much better to get the person to a hospital and keep him awake until professional help can be found.*

Can a person have an overdose from amphetamines?

Yes. An OD from speed is an over-amp. A person having an over-amp generally becomes very short winded and goes into convulsions. In a short period of time, the respiratory system becomes paralyzed, and death usually occurs in a matter of minutes. The other cause of death associated with over-amping is heart failure.

What first aid can be given a person who has over-amped?

Haste is of the essence. The person must be calmed down immediately. This can be done by getting him to lie down and talking him into taking slow deep breaths. Unlike the person having an overdose, the over-amp victim is usually conscious. Don't let him panic. Bathe the face with cool water. If there are depressants in the house, give him a couple. If he loses consciousness give mouth-to-mouth resuscitation. Apply it with external heart massage, if there is no pulse beat.

An over-amp is about ten times as dangerous as an overdose. An overdose can be fairly well controlled by keeping the person awake. An over-amp requires oxygen, and most people aren't equipped to deal with possible heart failure. Get the person to a hospital immediately. Even if he seems to be coming out of it, get him to a hospital.

I have heard that there are illnesses associated with drug usage. What are they?

The most common drug-related disease is hepatitis resulting from the use of unsanitary needles. Other problems common among drug users are malnutrition and tooth decay. The body becomes an easy target for colds and flu. For more information about drug-related illnesses, I suggest you contact your family doctor.

If a teenager goes to a doctor with a drug-related disease, does the doctor have to turn him over to the authorities?

Doctors are bound by their oaths not to reveal personal information. If a teen has a contagious disease such as VD or some forms of hepatitis, he turns that information over to the Public Health officials, for their use in compiling statistics and controlling the spread of diseases. To the best of my knowledge, the only thing a doctor is required by law to report is treatment of a gunshot wound.

What is this new LSD disease I have heard about?

At this point I can't find anyone who really knows what this disease is all about. There have been cases recently where people who used LSD four or five years ago have had visual problems and severe headaches. There hasn't been any definite answer as to whether or not this is a direct result of using LSD.

I've heard about LSD "bummers." My kids have denied using LSD, but is there a way to be prepared for the situation should it occur?

No. An acid bummer is completely unpredictable. The bummer might take the form of raving hysteria or quiet paranoia. There's no way of telling what the person is going to do. Physical restraint might be necessary, and if you can't handle it, call the fire department rescue squad or another ambulance service, advise them of the problem, and yell help. Unfortunately, the police roll on a lot of calls and the kid just might wind up in the prison ward of the hospital, but that's still better than anyone getting hurt or having the kid completely lose touch with reality.

My daughter had an LSD bummer. Will she need psychiatric help?

LSD is an extremely personal experience. There are two halves to the experience—the half caused by the drug, and the half caused by the personality. One individual may come down off an LSD bummer and be completely rational and coherent about the experience; another may have seen something that will send him straight off into never-never land. It wouldn't hurt for everyone using LSD, bummer or not, to see a psychiatrist. The only way to tell whether your daughter needs help is by the way she acts. Even if she seems normal now, that's still no assurance she'll stay that way.

What is a flashback?

A flashback can occur six months or six years or sixty years after having last used acid. A former LSD user is walking down the street, and suddenly the telephone poles turn into huge green snakes. Generally, flashbacks happen within a year or so after the use of acid, and they seem to decrease in frequency and intensity as time passes. Some people never have any, and others seem to never stop having them. It's another aspect of the LSD experience which science hasn't been able to explain or regulate.

I found enough dope to stock a pharmacy in the basement of our home. It would seem that our sweet, innocent, sixteen-year-old boy is the friendly neighborhood pusher. I'm tempted to call the cops. What is likely to happen if I do?

I can tell you exactly what will happen. A couple of cops will come out to the house, put all the dope in a box, handcuff the kid, and haul him away. The next step depends on your local laws. In some areas, a sixteen-year-old can be tried as an adult, depending on the severity of the charges. In most places, the kid would be taken to juvenile hall and released into your custody after being booked, if you so desired, or kept there until trial, if you don't.

At the trial, the kid will undoubtedly be found guilty and, again, depending on local laws, may be given probation and a suspended sentence, be given six months or longer in juvenile hall or a youth camp, be sent to a reform or training school or possibly even sent to prison.

Before making a decision of this nature I suggest you contact a lawyer and make certain how the law is upheld in your area. Texas, for example, goes hard on simple possession, but Southern California often gives probation for first-offense sales.

*We've decided that the only way to get our kid off
drugs is to turn him in. Do we just call
the police or what?*

You probably want the kid cured, not jailed.
You might look into Synanon, or Narcotics Anonymous, based on the program of Alcoholics
Anonymous. Perhaps your church has a drug
treatment center. A number of Catholic and Jew-
ish groups sponsor treatment centers in various
parts of the country. The United Way might be
able to help, or try your county health department.

*We have tried everything to get our child away
from drugs. Every time she leaves the
rehabilitation center, she goes straight back
to her pusher. Is there a point at which parents
are justified to give up?*

I suppose there must be. Sometimes a teenager
has to find his or her own strength to quit. When
nobody else is there to lean on or blame her
problems on, your daughter just might have to
face up to who she is. You can't live your kid's
life for her, and you can't be her crutch.

You shouldn't turn your back on her completely, solely out of frustration. The time for parents
to quit trying is when they honestly feel they have
done all they can to help, and recognize that
their teenager's problems are no longer their responsibility. After that, keep an open mind and be
willing to offer the kid the same amount of support you would to a close friend, and don't feel
you "owe" her anything more than that.

103

My teenage son has been heavily into drugs for about three years and wants out. For many reasons, we are going to have to do this thing by ourselves. How can drugs be combated without outside help?

Depending on what drugs your kid is using and how badly he's strung out, the physical kicking of the habit could range from easy to extremely difficult. If it turns out to be difficult, with his consent, lock him in a room with a bed and be prepared to clean up the mess.

After the withdrawal, the kid doesn't have to be watched every minute, but he does have to have every minute filled with a demanding physical or mental activity, especially if he has to spend hours alone while you are at work. An at-home job where he won't have to deal with people would be a good temporary solution. It is not only important that he be kept busy, but he also must be kept busy at something productive and financially profitable. This helps to develop a personal sense of value. School isn't the answer for the first few months of making the adjustment back into the real world. Schools are just as full of dope fiends as the streets are.

Moving to a new location where the kid doesn't know anyone would be of great value in the long run. If he really wants drugs, an addict can find them anywhere, but if he's really trying to give them up, it will be easier if he isn't exposed to any of his dope-fiend buddies. Your most important job will be to have a lot of long talks with your son, *helping him to find an alternative way of life.*

I read that use of speed is highly dangerous, but is not addictive. Is this true?

Speed is quite a trip when you're loaded on it, but then the drug starts to wear off. The first few times you take it, there aren't any bad after-effects—maybe a little tiredness, a little nausea. After using speed for a while, you get to taking more of it, more often, and staying up for longer and longer periods of time.

Confirmed addicts may stay awake for three weeks straight, not eating. They go through periods where they sit and slowly rock back and forth, their minds totally spaced out in hallucinations from lack of sleep. If one gets to the point of being a true speed freak, coming off the drug approaches insanity. When you're stoned, you can't feel pain. When the speed eases off, you start to feel the effects from days of no food or sleep: the gnawing in your belly, the ache of abused muscles, and toothaches. And all it takes to put an end to all that pain is a couple of little pills, a half teaspoon of powder, or a half cc of fluid in the veins. Anything that would make you consider murdering your granny to get another fix is addictive, despite what the "clinical experts" say to the contrary.

Our teenager doesn't have any problems with drugs, but he seems to be drinking quite a bit. Where can he go for help?

Suggest Alcoholics Anonymous. The person with a drinking problem doesn't have to live on skid row or sleep behind billboards or be over the hill to qualify for help.

If your son is having drinking problems and wants to quit, he'll find a lot of support and help from other young people, teenagers included, who found their drinking was interfering with their living.

My teen had a drinking problem, but it seems to be under control, now that we've talked about it. Do teenagers have the same "falling off the wagon" problems as adults do?

Adults seem to feel that teenagers are members of some foreign race, but they're not. Teenagers today are informed, sophisticated, and aware. Teenagers encounter the same problems the adult establishment does, and some new ones, for that matter. It's no easier for a teenager dependent on alcohol to give it up than it is for an adult.

Our daughter spent the past two years going through hell. She left home at seventeen and was picked up six months ago for prostitution, sick with hepatitis, and strung out on drugs. She was placed in a treatment center as part of her probation, but will be coming home soon. We love her and would like to know if there is anything special we can do to help her readjust?

Don't do anything *special*. Doing things special would only amplify the feeling that she has a lot of readjustment to do by making her aware of her outsider status. In other words, don't treat her like a freak.

It's not wise to pretend she's been in a regular

hospital with an illness, but don't treat her like an ex-con either. Avoid acting as though she were a victim of circumstances that weren't her fault. Prostitution is a crime, and she got busted. It's as simple as that. By the same token don't throw a lot of guilt on her. The courts must have realized there were mitigating factors, or she would be in prison. Avoid dredging up the past and trying to find the reasons for her problems. That's all behind her now. Just hang loose and treat the subject as matter of factly as possible.

I'm sure there will be someone at the treatment center, possibly a therapist, whom you will be able to discuss these things with before your daughter comes home. The counselor will be able to fill you in on your daughter's problems and treatment, as well as how her treatment should be continued once she gets home.

Our oldest child is in a drug treatment center. Should our other children, ages fifteen and sixteen, be told the truth about what's going on?

They probably already know, but it would be a good idea to discuss it with them. This is a family problem. Protecting the other kids from the problem won't bring about the kind of stable family relationship that helps combat drug usage. The experience of the oldest child may help the younger ones to avoid drugs completely.

Our daughter is pregnant and took drugs for the first four months. We are bearing enough shame as it is. Does the doctor have to know?

God, yes! It may already be too late. Get this

information to the doctor immediately. And one more thing, leave that girl and her doctor alone. I would strongly recommend you get professional help for the whole family, if you really are concerned.

What can parents do to help the police get rid of dope pushers?

In some cities the police have a program called Turn In Pushers (TIP). They have a number anyone can call to pass on information. The caller doesn't have to give his name, and all information is confidential. Information can be based on a mere suspicion. The experts will take it from there. Because of a system of code names used for callers, if a conviction is obtained, the caller can receive a cash reward without the police ever knowing his true identity.

You may want to talk to your local police and city council to see if such a program could be set up locally. With everyone in the city a potential informer and with the cash incentive to lure the pusher's associates, drugs seem to die out in a hurry.

Chapter 6

JESUS CHRIST AND OTHER SUPERSTARS

What is a "Jesus Freak"?

A "Jesus Freak" is the name currently being applied to the group of young, and not so young, people who have found a place for themselves in the revival of a Pentecostal religion. The basic tenet of the Jesus movement is that after a person confesses and asks the Spirit of Jesus Christ to forgive him for his sins and completely take over his life, he will be accepted by Christ as one of His new followers. This transformation is usually a dramatic event which may include garbled speech (speaking in "tongues") and "Holy Rolling".

The Jesus Freaks attempt to exemplify the life of Christ, some moving into communes in an effort to be "no part of this world." Their aim is to completely shed their old personalities and become a living image of Jesus.

What's the big lure of the Jesus movement?

I don't know if there is a "lure". A lot of kids today are attracted to spirituality. It isn't unique to be concerned with these matters; most of us, at one time or another, seek the answers to man's purpose on earth, the meaning of life and death, and the mysteries of creation.

The kids are not willing to accept the answers their parents offer at face value and on blind faith alone. The Jesus movement has going for it a new way of expressing religious beliefs. A lot of teenagers don't buy the pomp and ceremony of traditional faiths. The Jesus movement is an activist religion. While churches and synagogues conduct services on one day of the week, the Jesus movement promotes twenty-four-hour-a-day religion. They live it, rather than practice it.

With the constant barrage of earthshaking events reported daily in newspapers and on television, many people, especially the teenagers, feel that this society is unhealthy. Members of the Jesus movement feel they can completely withdraw from the reality of murders, deleted expletives, corruption, and hush money, and form a new religious order of their own where such problems never occur.

What goes on in the communes I've heard about?

There are hundreds of communes, and lifestyles differ according to leadership, commune goals, location, and financial backing.

In many communes, the members are trying to establish values different from those of traditional society, and remove themselves from the mainstream in order to accomplish their goals. The members may have spiritual goals, want to experiment with utopian concepts, believe strongly in community living and extended family relationships, or want to live a simpler, rural existence. In some instances, radios, television, magazines, and newspapers are banned.

Most communes are supported in part by outside contributions from wealthy sympathizers and in part by their own labor, such as farming, leather crafts, and other small industries. Overall, it isn't an easy life. Many have strict codes regarding dress, relationships, and morals.

In religious communes, the members may spend much of their time in directed Bible study and prayer. The city communes are often better off financially than their country cousins. They try and integrate themselves into the community, often the poorer sections of a city, and to reach people through prayer.

To the best of my knowledge, there aren't any strange occurrences in the majority of religious communes. However, there are some which have strict rules. In one instance, documented in a woman's magazine, a teenage girl was required to give up her child because of a commune regulation that all children be raised at a central location by selected members within the commune. She left the group rather than give up her child.

I've heard that when a person joins one of these communes he's required to turn over all his material possessions and encouraged to bring

along everything of value he can get his
hands on. This sounds like some kind of racket
to me. Is it?

It looks that way to a lot of people, especially
the parents of the kids who want to join. It is
true that in some communes there are regulations
against retaining personal property. If it is a con,
it's done beautifully. The joiner feels he is con-
tributing to the welfare of the whole, and, since
he is a part of the whole, he isn't losing anything.
The people who are signing over bonds and bank
accounts are doing so completely of their own
free will.

Perhaps any person, regardless of age, would
benefit by spending a year or two in a religious
commune, but I don't think a teenager has the
maturity or experience to make a decision to turn
over all of his worldly possessions. What if he
needed money to attend college or go into business
later? Or simply get a job and start a family?
And no teenager should expect his parents to do-
nate possessions on his behalf.

There's no doubt the communes need financial
help to remain open, but before making contributions, it would be wise to find out how much
financial help the commune is willing to give its
members who decide to leave.

My sixteen-year-old ran away last year after
talking about joining one of the Jesus
communes. How do I locate her?

There is a man named Ted Patrick in San
Diego, California, who spends much of his time
helping parents find children who have joined

112

the Jesus movement. Mr. Patrick had the problem hit home when his own child joined the movement. His program includes locating the child and helping reorient him or her into a more moderate practice of religion.

Mr. Patrick would be more than happy to discuss this problem with parents. His home phone number is: 714/479-4773.

I managed to pull my teenager out of a Jesus commune. He had been existing on garbage when I found him. It cost me nearly $2,000. Now, every time I get him straightened out, one of those bearded nuts shows up preaching hell, fire, and damnation and ruins the whole thing. What can I do?

It sounds like your teenager needs the services of a minister, rabbi, or priest, who can remove the fears and guilts this kind of preaching implants. Perhaps, he could benefit from psychological counseling as well.

The object of religion, to my way of thinking, is peace and love, not fear. That's the biggest objection I have to this movement.

As far as the "bearded nuts" are concerned, it could be possible to have a restraining order placed against the group as a whole. A lawyer or marshall would be able to give you additional information. Another piece of ammunition available to you would be to talk at length with one of the "bearded nuts" and find out exactly what it is you are fighting. One word of caution: Don't lose your temper. Not only is it against the law to hit him, threats could also get you into serious trouble.

My kids are involved with a group which operates out of a storefront and is involved with public service projects. Is this part of the Jesus movement?

Yes. The three largest groups are the Campus Crusade for Christ, Teen Challenge, and the Children of God. According to Peter Michelmore in *Back to Jesus,* the Children of God have been catching all the flak. Teen Challenge is run by the Reverend David Wilkerson. His group started out working with teenage gangs, but branched into teenage drug and delinquency problems. Campus Crusade is concerned with evangelism on the campus, and also engages in service projects.

There are also many smaller groups devoted to rehabilitating drug addicts and runaways. These groups are dedicated to practicing Christianity twenty-four hours a day, and once a community gets used to their unorthodox approach to religion, they could prove to be a great asset to their neighbors.

Wasn't this whole thing started by the play "Jesus Christ Superstar"?

No.

I saw one of my teenager's friends wearing a robe, his hair in a scalp lock, and beating a tambourine on one of the busiest corners downtown? What's he gotten himself into?

It sounds like the Hare Krishna movement. The members live by a very disciplined code of laws. They are a self-supporting group who live in a communal arrangement, financed by farming and making incense, which they sell, legally, on the street to the beat of tambourines and chants. They are very well-mannered and clean people, if a somewhat strange sight.

It is a difficult religion to observe; the members are extremely dedicated. They allow no drugs or other stimulants in their community, believe strongly in marriage, and practice sexual relations only for procreation.

They emphasize spiritual awareness, sanctity of life, and peace. There is a great appeal to young people in a religion that rejects materialism to such a great extent.

My kids want to attend a meeting of the Krishna group, but I'm against it. I think they're a bunch of troublemakers, and I don't want my kids influenced by them.

If the kids have expressed an interest in the group, they are already influenced to a certain extent. The Hare Krishna are not troublemakers in any sense of the word. If you don't want your kids influenced by attitudes of peace and brotherhood, don't let them go.

Actually, they are a fascinating group. Their festivals are both colorful and entertaining. Exploring foreign cultures, religions, and life-styles is a good experience for everyone. Not only would I let the kids go, I'd go myself. If you still feel they are troublemakers after seeing and talking with them firsthand, discuss your feelings with the kids. It may not resolve anything, but it will bring you closer together.

My sixteen-year-old has become interested in the "Chariots of the Gods" cult. Is there a religion connected with it?

It's more of a religious opinion. Some people have spent a lot of time researching various holy books to locate passages which can be interpreted to have a subtle, scientific meaning. For instance, some believe that when Moses climbed the mount to receive the Ten Commandments and was told to wait until a horn blew before approaching the mountain top, it was because the area was too hot for life, after the landing of a star ship.

Every religion has its references to fiery objects in the sky and supernatural voices promising a return to earth, which will result in the salvation of mankind. The Eskimo's claim that their ancestors were brought to the snowy land in the belly of a great silver bird. Most religions have a god or angel who appeared in some sort of airborne chariot. Even Greek and Roman myths have their flying super-beings.

To some persons, these references point the way to a race of ancient astronauts who plan to one day return and remove the plagues from earth by means of an advanced technology. They feel that one day the "Ship" will return and fulfill all the ancient prophecies of all religions. The people holding this belief are sometimes referred to as "Spacers".

Our fifteen-year-old has become involved with witchcraft. Don't these people sexually exploit young people in their strange ceremonies?

Most witchcraft groups are probably harmless,

although there might be exceptions. There are ancient rituals in witchcraft which demand sacrificing a virgin, but how many people would go along with abducting and murdering a young girl? More common is the sacrificing of virginity to the devil or other occult spirits. A very sick group could coerce a girl into forsaking her virginity or require her to submit to intercourse with all the male members of the group.

While most members of witchcraft cults are sane, in any group, especially one with a history of bizarre rituals, there might be some nuts. If you think there is anything unhealthy going on, get your kid out of there fast and notify the police. They'll at least investigate.

I've heard that Manson and his followers engaged in Satanic religious orgies. Is this true?

There has been much written about what went on behind the gates of the Spahn Movie Ranch in the summer of 1969, but it still remains a matter of conjecture. The media made much out of Manson's supposed occult powers, but the only way to know for sure would be to have been there.

I talked with a person who was at the ranch in 1968, long before the Tate murders. He said Manson spent most of his time passing out drugs to the girls. Manson supposedly is a very intelligent man, and played "mind games" with the girls, who often wound up in the bedroom. My informer's experience with the Manson family was a prolonged orgy, one of sex and drugs. He claimed never to have seen any witchcraft, although Manson did have a strange, hypnotic way of looking at people that frightened them.

Another person, who considers himself a warlock, alleged that several female members of the Manson family, who were later involved in the murders, had lived with him. He stated they were involved in witchcraft before their association with Manson began.

How can a parent recognize a dangerous involvement before it reaches the point it did in California?

It's difficult. There were some similarities in the California teenagers' backgrounds. They hadn't seen their parents for quite a while. They all had long histories of drug or street involvement. They had a central base of operations at the ranch, away from the eyes of parents and the law. If a parent has some influence and communication with his or her teenager, it is less likely he or she will stray so far away from traditional mores.

Are satanic groups protected by the law, or are we free to have them run out of town?

Nobody is free to have anybody else run out of town. If there is the need to remove an offensive element from the community, the police can do it quite effectively. If there is such a group, but they haven't broken any laws, there is the letters-to-the-editor column in your local newspaper. Most television and radio stations and newspapers thrive on such news and would be happy to look into any group which might be harmful.

All religions are protected by the Constitution, and that includes Catholics, Jews, Buddhists,

Protestants, witches, and those who worship cracks in the sidewalk.

Does early religious training help kids establish moral values?

That would depend on whose answer you were willing to accept—a psychiatrist's, a religious leader's, or mine. Sometimes religious training can fill a person with all kinds of fears and guilts.

A well-balanced person from a well-balanced family can benefit from religious instruction. If kids have learned a particular set of religious beliefs and values while growing up, they will be able to draw upon this faith, during difficult times, if they so choose.

My seventeen-year-old has declared himself to be an athiest. I'm disturbed by it, but how can I fight it?

The way to fight it is not to fight it at all. Don't discuss religion with your teenager every time you feel you have to, but be ready to discuss it any time he might want to. Bone up on religion and science, so you'll know what you're talking about. Keep the discussion lively and good humored.

A lot of people go through a period in which they have many questions, but no answers. It is natural for young people to doubt everything they are told to be true, until they have the experience and insight to establish their own beliefs. Don't worry about it, and don't force the kid into becoming a confirmed athiest by pressing the issue.

Our 17-year-old daughter just told us that she is tired of being force-fed our "straight world" values. We were shocked by her attitude, but we didn't fully understand what she meant. Do you?

I can take a guess. The fact that this was a sudden outburst says a lot. She probably has a problem that doesn't fall into the conventional bounds of the older generation, and she doesn't know how to handle it. It is doubtful that the parents of today's teens had to decide on whether or not to take an acid trip with their boyfriend or girl friend or whether or not to agree to a trial marriage. It could be that a problem along these lines is bothering her, and all she has to go on are the moral standards which you had given her.

The biggest hassle between parents and kids these days is the fact that the times have changed so drastically. Neither parents nor teens have a clear understanding of what it is to be a member of the other generation. Your generation is the "straight world" in which drug and free-love problems are not supposed to exist. (A lot of teenagers, and perhaps parents, would be surprised to learn how small the difference actually is.)

Talk to her about her values and the values of that world which is not "straight." Think about what you have told her in the past and try to see how your clear-cut black and white thinking might add to the confusion of a person raised in a shades-of-gray world. Hang in there, love her, and see if all of you can't come to a better understanding of each other.

Our religion believes in infant baptism. Our children haven't baptized our grandchildren, and we are quite upset. How can we get them to see things our way?

All you can do is explain your position, unemotionally, to your kids, and in this way show them why you feel this issue is so important. If your teenagers can't see the point of your beliefs, try to accept it.

We had this problem come up in our family when our first son was born. My wife's family stated their position, and we stated ours. Our sons still haven't been baptized. If, in the future, the boys, themselves, decide to be baptized, I'll be proud to attend the services.

My problem isn't with religion, it's with fanaticism. My son spent six months in jail where a racial problem developed involving a Black Panther-type organization and a group of American Nazis. His bigotry is making me sick. What can I do?

Bigotry can arise from bad experiences. There is a lot of racial trouble in the world, and it is magnified in jail. Joining racial groups in jail is often the only way to survive. The few people who can get away with having friends of other races are the hard-core cons whose reputations forbid any retaliation from other prisoners. Unless a prisoner is feared, he doesn't dare act as though he tolerates other races.

A bigoted attitude isn't learned or ingrained in jail, it's shoved down a person's throat. The stories and the experiences of a prisoner (of any race) begin to make sense, and the bigotry seems valid.

After the person is released, the prejudice, which began as a survival tactic and later became a truth, is difficult to part with. It's similar to the problem of a soldier who has spent two years killing Orientals and suddenly finds himself back home where Orientals are not enemies. It's hard to stop hating. Just as the soldier has to be retrained, so does the prisoner.

The way to do this is to make your son aware of why he had to become a bigot in the first place, and why it is no longer necessary. Point out the difference between two races in confinement who are sworn enemies and forced to act out their hatred and the same two races living peacefully in a community, learning from each other and getting along on the basis of mutual hopes and dreams.

In discussing prejudices, make the kid prove what he says against another race. His evidence will be based on what went on within the prison walls. Then show him how his facts don't apply on the outside. Keep calm and talk facts instead of preaching. He'll eventually come around.

Our sixteen-year-old daughter has practically made a religion based on a trinity of David Cassidy, Donny Osmond, and Michael Jackson. Her biggest goal in life is to spend the coming summer as a "groupie". Will this pass, or should I give her a good lecture?

Better she should be infatuated with pictures of recording stars than with some twenty-year-old hoodlum. First there was Sinatra, then there was

Elvis. Now there's Cassidy, Osmond, and Jackson. Next year there will undoubtedly be somebody else. As long as there are sexy male singers, there will be infatuated teenage girls.

Being a groupie is something else. This involves traveling around the country and being available if the singer should happen to take notice. By the time summer has rolled around, the problem will probably have ceased to exist. Don't let it hassle you. If she is still persistent, come summer, yes, try to talk her out of it.

Our daughter is seventeen and is going with a guy devoted to one of those Eastern religions. I understand they view their women on a level somewhat lower than cattle. Is it good for an American girl to be treated this way?

I would suggest that if you have questions regarding the guy's religion, ask him. That's the only way to find out what his beliefs are. Secondly, if his beliefs do hold women in an inferior position, let your daughter decide for herself if that's the kind of life she wants.

My 16-year-old spends most of his time alone in his room chanting in front of a picture. He also meditates. Is he crazy or is this a phase?

It's undoubtedly a phase. The chanting, according to the Hindu religion, is supposed to form rhythmic waves which bring about a specific reaction, depending on the chant and to whom it is directed. The chanting is supposed to contribute to the well-being of the chanter. I wouldn't worry about it. A lot kids are attracted to Eastern religions.

My twenty-year-old daughter has been living with a bunch of hippies for about a year. They practice some sort of homespun religion which includes group marriage. To me, it's just a way of rationalizing swapping sexual partners.
How can I convince her that this is an unhealthy way to live?

It is very hard to understand people who live by codes we have always regarded as immoral. There are ideas my generation has developed which I don't even pretend to understand. I guess everybody has to find a way of life that they can live, and if they don't they'll never be happy.

Today, there seem to be more young people who are willing to throw conventions aside and strike out in search of a new way of life. In a way, it's hard not to respect them, but it's almost impossible to understand them.

I can't explain how people might validly rationalize group marriage. In all probability, they do see it as something legitimate and having value. For some people, this sort of thing might work, but for the majority, traditional marriage proves best. The high rate of divorce and adultery in this country, unfortunately, is sighted as evidence that marriage as we know it doesn't work. I'm not defending group marriage; I'm happily and devotedly married and we've been together for five years. To many people, group marriage is immoral. To others, group marriage is a perfectly valid life-style.

What I'm trying to point out is that different

people have different ideas on moral behavior. I don't know how to convince other people they are wrong. It is especially difficult if their beliefs are in conjunction with what they hold to be religious truths or a sociological experiment. The only thing to do is promote love and explain your own position. In that way, it is possible your daughter will understand some of the values in your way of life.

With all these exciting and colorful new religious cults, how can a church or synagogue interest young people in a youth program?

Give the kids a place to meet. One Los Angeles church established a youth center which became very popular. The center had three rooms: one for records, pool, and ping-pong; another for chess, checkers, and cards; and a third for dancing.

On Friday nights, the room for dancing, which had a small stage, was converted into a coffee house by setting up tables and chairs, and dramatically lighting the room with candles. Local talent was invited to perform. A seventy-five-cent donation was requested at the door. The evening's collection was split amongst the entertainers. Occasionally, a name performer would appear and really stir up excitement. Two or three young adults or young married couples served as chaperones.

Another activity that attracts kids is a rap session. Kids love to talk and exchange complaints. They'll often open up more away from their parents. Group excursions, sponsored by the synagogue or church, are also of interest, but be original. Try surfing, a beach party or hikes, trips to historical places, or rock concerts. Some groups allow the kids to decide which activities to pursue at monthly meetings. The kids will get involved, if given the opportunity.

Chapter 7

MOM, I'VE BEEN BUSTED

I overheard one of my kids tell a friend he'd been "popped" and had an "F.I." filled out on him. I know this had something to do with the police. Is it serious?

The term "popped," in the context you overheard it, meant stopped and questioned by a policeman. This can also be called a "roust," although roust usually implies an unwarranted questioning. Rousts are usually made on known criminals, to warn them the police are aware of their presence and possibly as a harrassment to get them out of the area. Popped is also used to mean caught in a crime and arrested.

An "F.I." is a Field Interrogation Card. Field interrogation is the on-the-spot questioning of a suspicious person. The person's name, address, description, license number, make and color of car, and the suspect's explanation of what he had been doing in the area are requested. This information is usually recorded on a three-by-five card along with the date, location, time, and the name of the inquiring officer.

These cards are held on file at the station. In the event a crime took place in the area on that date and at that time, the police have a partial record of people in the vicinity who either fit the description of suspects or are possible witnesses. A field interrogation is in no way serious, and it is not placed on any type of record of criminal activity.

An example that comes to mind is one night when my cousin and I had lost our way near Malibu Lake in Southern California. As it happened, the driveway we chose to turn around in was that of a construction company plagued by burglaries. Coincidentally, a sheriff was behind us, and when we pulled in the driveway of the closed construction yard, he regarded it as a suspicious act and pulled us over. Our explanation was valid, but he still filled out F.I. cards on us, in case anyone had spotted a red Mustang like ours in the area when the burglaries had occurred. The police usually don't fill out an F.I. unless there has been some suspicious behavior, but almost anyone can appear suspicious. Don't worry about it.

When the police have enough reason to stop a kid, why don't they inform his parents?

Sometimes they do. If the kid was doing something unusual, say cutting through a fence, to get across a field, chances are the police would take

128

him to the station and have his parents come get him. Even this situation shouldn't cause undue concern.

If a teenager has a record of being stopped by police, sooner or later they will notify the parents. It's so easy to get stopped, most of the time the police accept the kid's explanation and let it go at that.

Our town has a ten P.M. curfew for teenagers. Should we let our kids attend movies or other events which end after curfew?

The extent to which a curfew regulation is enforced varies from place to place. Curfew laws are basically designed to protect teenagers, and keep them out of trouble.

Contrary to popular belief, the police are not an extension of a Fascist state. They have no objections to teens being out at night if they have definite plans and legitimate activities. This includes travel to and from movies, bowling, and, especially, school affairs, such as sports events, or dances and even includes stopping for a hamburger and a cola on the way home.

What is frowned upon is stopping for a joint or a couple of pills on the way home from a happy night of smashing car windshields and setting fire to the school. In some towns, where there has been trouble, a parent or another adult *must* escort the kids home personally. Your local police will be able to tell you if this is the case in your area. Also check the curfew regulations in neighboring towns where your teens may go for entertainment.

What happens if a teenager is picked up after curfew?

In most cases, nothing. Curfew violations aren't a crime. The police take the teenager to the station and call the parents to come pick him or her up. The teenager is questioned briefly, but that's about it.

A shop girl at the drugstore informed me my fourteen-year-old was caught shoplifting, but the store manager let her go with a lecture and a warning. My daughter hasn't said a word. Should I bring it up?

Yeah. Shoplifting is serious. Obviously, the store manager felt the matter could be dropped and that there wouldn't be a repeat performance, but I would not let it end there.

First, have a talk with the manager of the store and find out exactly what happened. By the way, this is nothing to be embarrassed about. It happens all the time, and if the manager let your daughter go, it sounds like he is a very understanding fellow.

When you bring the subject up at home, remember it's not the Great Train Robbery. Don't blow it up out of proportion. On the other hand, the girl should be made aware that shoplifting is a crime, the kind of crime people go to jail for. Also make sure you point out that the manager didn't tell you. Having the manager tell tales behind the kid's back could create resentment, not just against the manager, but against adults in general.

After you've discussed the issue, drop it. The

whole family doesn't have to know, and the girl shouldn't feel you are suspicious every time she goes to the store or brings home a gift from someone.

My daughter has been coming home with clothes and cosmetics that have obviously been shoplifted. She seems to think the police don't lock girls up for small things like this.

First, call the police and ask how many girls in your daughter's age group were arrested last year for shoplifting. The figures will be surprising.

Next, if that doesn't shock her into her senses, see if a tour of a women's prison is possible. If that doesn't work, the only thing that will stop her is being caught. If she is caught, unfortunately, she's going to find out just how quick the police arrest anyone who commits a crime.

My seventeen-year-old boy got a ticket for running a red light. Are traffic laws different for juveniles?

California is fairly representative of the nation, and the laws here are different for juveniles. A teenager who gets a ticket has to appear in a special court with his parents. No one I know ever beat a juvenile ticket in California, although I'm sure it must happen. Most juvenile traffic violations don't carry a fine. Instead the kid's license is suspended for anywhere from fourteen days to several years, depending on the seriousness of the offense.

My sixteen-year-old drives a '65 Pontiac with a custom, metal-flake paint job, chrome wheels and lowered suspension. He's been written up four times for moving violations. I think the cops are picking on my boy because he has never been stopped driving my stock Chevy. Can I make a complaint?

If the tickets have been issued by four different policemen, I don't think a complaint would be valid. The police may watch such cars more carefully, or your son may drive your Chevy more carefully.

If your local police headquarters has a public affairs office, visit it by all means. If you can, find out if the officers have been singling the boy out. There may be more to this story than meets the eye. Make sure your boy is obeying all the laws.

If the police are harrassing your son, the visit to the public affairs office will probably put a stop to it. If your son gets another ticket, take it to court and inform the public affairs officer you talked with, to get his viewpoint. He will be able to obtain the complete story from the arresting officer.

Our eighteen-year-old didn't pay a ticket, and an arrest warrant came to the house. What should we do?

Now your teenager is facing two charges: the original charge on the ticket, which can still be fought, and the additional charge of not appearing.

In California this second charge carries a penalty of up to six months in jail and/or a $500 fine. This charge can also be fought, but first there will be an arraignment where the defendant will enter a plea and bail will be set. Since the defendant didn't show up on his promise to appear on the original ticket, bail is usually an amount that would cover the probable fine if he is found guilty.

There are few excuses accepted for failure to appear. One would be that the defendant was in jail on another charge at the time. Another possible excuse would be if the defendant thought, in all honesty and for good reason, that someone else had taken care of the ticket.

An excuse of illness, forgetfulness, pressing personal problems, etc. is the same as a guilty plea. The courts just won't go for it. The thing to do now is go to court and, unless the kid has a valid reason for not having appeared, pay the fine.

What happens if a teenager is picked up for a traffic warrant?

He is taken to jail, in handcuffs. He is searched, fingerprinted, photographed, his property taken, and he is thrown in a cell. Within seventy-two hours, not counting weekends and holidays, he is taken to court and charged. It is a formal arrest and goes on his permanent record.

Is there any way of getting someone out of jail before they go to court on this charge?

Yes. Bail on this charge is usually placed on the face of the warrant itself. Bail can be posted at the police station at any time before the arraignment. The prisoner will then be released.

What is bail?

Bail is a sum of money which is held instead of a person. The best way of explaining it is to use, for example, a traffic ticket. When a person gets a ticket, it is actually an arrest. He signs the ticket, promising to appear on the date and at the time specified and is released by the policeman, rather than jailed until the time of trial. Instead of going to trial, the person can post bail. This is commonly thought to be the paying of the fine, but it is not.

On the day of the trial the judge reads the charge, asks if the defendant is present, checks to see if bail has been posted and if it has, he then forfeits the bail, finds the defendant guilty, and fines him the amount of the bail.

In other types of arrests, the prisoner is released on an amount of money the court feels he will not want to forfeit. In this way, the courts are assured of his appearance at the trial.

What is a bail bondsman?

A bondsman is a man who arranges bail for people who have been arrested. The person who is seeking bail for a friend or relative puts up ten percent of the total, and the bondsman puts up the rest. When the prisoner shows up for trial, the bondsman's money is refunded. The ten percent is kept by the bondsman as his fee for arranging the bail. In the event the person doesn't show, the person who arranged for the bondsman's services is then responsible for the full amount of the bail.

Our child is nineteen and was arrested for selling drugs. The bail is $1,500. Is it wise to have a bondsman arrange it?

If you have no other way of posting the bail, what other choice is there? The only other possible course of action would be to talk with the lawyer and see if the court will release the kid on an "O.R.", which is on his "own recognizance," or on his word that he'll appear for trial. It isn't unusual for a judge to release someone, even on a charge of this nature, if it is a first offense and there is a record of stability in the family. Another alternative is for the court to reduce the amount of bail. Talk with the lawyer.

If none of these approaches work, check with a bondsman. It costs nothing to talk to one, and some bondsmen make arrangements for the ten percent to be paid out on time, in trade for holding the pink slip on a car or something else of value. There are lots of ways he'll help you work it out.

Our teen was picked up for possession of marijuana. It was a first offense. What is the usual outcome of this charge?

There is absolutely no way of telling. There are a couple of states that still hold life sentences for this offense. In California, the kid would probably have his hand slapped and be sent home. In many states, the average sentence is about two years, if any time is done at all, with probation running a close second.

The attitude toward possession of grass is slowly changing, even if the laws aren't. Think of some good reasons why the judge should grant probation. If your teenager gets a job, enrolls in a school, performs volunteer work for the community, or seeks drug counseling, these are all ways a teenager can display a positive change in attitude. Employers, teachers, community leaders, and counselors can be called into court as his character witnesses. Also, talk with the lawyer and find out if one judge is more lenient than another. This is a common procedure and sometimes can make a world of difference.

Do the police ever make "deals"?

Every time I hear about police making deals, I think of Jack Webb snapping the handcuffs on a prisoner and saying, "We don't make deals, fella, you're going to jail!"

In all the time I spent on the street, I never once met a cop who wouldn't make deals. The deals they make are tighter than a finance company contract.

It works like this: The kid who's been busted, generally for drugs, gives the police the name of his connection. Then the police give the kid some marked money (the serial numbers on the money have been recorded). The kid buys some more drugs, gives them to the police, and the police arrest the connection with the marked money on his person, proving the sale. Later, the kid has to testify in court against the connection, that is unless the connection makes his own deal against his connection.

A detective once told me that good police work consists of the detectives sitting around the squad room drinking coffee and waiting for someone to come in and tell them who committed the crime.

Our eighteen-year-old was just picked up for the third time for sale and possession of dangerous drugs. The lawyer bills are killing us. Should we keep being played for fools?

I wouldn't. The kid is an adult, and you aren't required to come up with a lawyer. Let the court supply a public defender, and let the kid take his chances.

What should a parent do if he can't afford a lawyer?

In a criminal charge, the courts can appoint a public defender who will handle your case. If you don't earn over $4,500 annually, your local Legal Aid Society will take the case. If all else fails, contact the American Civil Liberties Union for further information.

Our seventeen-year-old was arrested for petty theft, but the lawyer said she could probably manage to get probation. What will this mean?

Probation is usually granted on a guilty plea by the defendant. The defendant is given a sentence consisting of time and/or a fine; then the sentence is suspended, and a period of probation is set up. For instance, the sentence might be one year, suspended, and three years probation. For three years, the court, through the probation office, will keep an eye on the person's behavior.

If the defendant violates the terms of his probation, he is called up before a board, and the incident is reviewed. The board will decide whether he should be allowed to continue on probation or be confined for a part or all of his original sentence. If he serves out his probation without any more problems, that's the end of the matter.

If a teenager completes his probation to the satisfaction of the court, will the arrest always be on his record?

A juvenile record can be sealed by court order for the protection of kids who got into trouble before they were old enough to know better. The process has to be handled through a lawyer, but it is fairly uncomplicated and not too expensive.

What is the difference between probation and parole?

Probation is given to someone whose sentence has been suspended. A person on parole has served a part of his sentence in jail or prison and then been released. A person in California can be sentenced to "five to life" for felony armed robbery. He may be eligible for parole in two or three years, and be on parole for eight to ten years. The conditions of parole are similar to those for probation.

One of my kid's friends snatched a purse downtown the other day. He wasn't caught, but I recognized him. Should I call the police, go to the kid's parents, or what?

That's a rugged decision to have to make. A citizen is required by law to furnish information to the police about any crime he or she might have witnessed. You're under a legal obligation to turn the kid in. Whether or not you do it is another matter. What would you want done if you were the parents of a thief? How will the kid's parents react?

In your position, I'd call the kid's parents and tell them exactly what happened. My second call would be to the police.

Our son is sixteen and is running around with a bunch of hoodlums. Should we forbid any further association with this bunch, or is there a better way of getting him away from them?

Forbidding him to associate with the gang won't work. Kids join gangs for a number of reasons, and you don't have to be an expert to understand them. Gangs are exciting, and their ranks are filled with kids who can't seem to get it together with socially acceptable groups. The best way of getting a kid away from a bad element is to help him find something worthwhile to do.

There are many alternatives. Try to encourage him to take a part-time job, which will help build his self-esteem. Does he have any interests you could promote—an ability to draw? He could take art classes. A talent for music? He could take guitar lessons or join a local rock group. Sports? If he doesn't take an active interest in group participation sports, perhaps swimming, surfing, judo, or kung fu would appeal to him.

Many churches have excellent youth groups, which sponsor interesting outings and weekly social events. A "hard" guy would consider this kind of activity a little tame, perhaps, but these teenagers do know how to have fun. For shy teenagers, and even tough guys are shy, it's hard to mix at first in large groups. If a teenager can be convinced that the first two or three times are the most uncomfortable, it will help him over the hump, and he'll be able to enjoy himself.

Spending a lot of time with the kid on your own will help. The conversation is bound to roll around to the reasons gang life is so appealing to him. Don't harp on the subject. If the kid has to be led into it, do it slowly.

Our son is almost twenty and has joined a real tough motorcycle gang. From what I read, once you're in a gang like that, there is no getting out. Can we hope he'll ever return to a normal way of life?

I've read similar articles. Sensationalism sells. The writers of these stories obviously don't know the first thing about bikers.

The truth of the matter is that bike gangs, for the most part, are composed of guys and girls that love motorcycles, not the little Japanese transportation bikes, but the big, American-built cycles. Bikers are rowdy; they drink heavily; and they get involved in barroom brawls. They stick to themselves, and generally don't cause trouble outside their own group.

In order to join a bike gang in the first place, a guy has to have a reputation as a hard case. This reputation alone wins him the respect of the other bikers. When the time comes to "hang up your colors," there isn't any hassle about it. Generally, guys just drift off, but there are times when the whole club turns out for a "retirement party" for a member who is getting married or settling down. Part of this information comes from personal experience, and part from a "retired" Hell's Angel. Angels are, of course, supposed to be the elite among outlaw bikers, and the toughest club to get out of.

How can pressure be brought against a gang that is causing trouble in the community?

Go to the police and complain for a start. Of course, the police are unable to do anything unless there has been an offense committed and the citizen is willing to press charges. A citizen's group is especially effective in applying pressure to get the district attorney's office and the city council involved. They can see to it that police patrols are stepped up in the area, and, if it's a bike gang, the police will check every machine for stolen parts or illegal equipment. The police can do quite a bit to harrass the gang and still be entirely within the law, by strictly enforcing drinking laws and checking gang members every night for traffic warrants.

My son was picked up with three older boys in a stolen car. He didn't know the car was stolen, but he was at the wheel when the police stopped them. The other three boys were charged with joy riding, but my boy was hit for grand auto theft. None of the other boys have offered to help, and my son refuses to "cop out" on his friends. What should I do?

Go down to the police station and talk with the

detective who is handling the case. Tell him exactly what your son has told you. The police don't want to lock up innocent people, and, in a case like this, they will do everything possible to get at the truth. Anybody who would let a friend go to jail for them is no friend at all. Your son must be convinced of this.

My seventeen-year-old was arrested for an armed robbery which he had nothing to do with. He can't prove that he spent the night in question alone at the beach. Two witnesses have identified him. Naturally, he wants to plead not guilty, but the public defender says he doesn't have a prayer. Armed robbery carries a penalty of two to ten years in prison in this state. The public defender told us the district attorney will accept a guilty plea to a lesser charge of grand theft which usually carries two years in a work camp. With time off, my son should do about nine months. Can this be happening in America? What can we do?

It's happening in America more and more. This is what is known as plea bargaining. Court trials take time, and a jury costs money. Ten years in a prison costs the state more than nine months in a work camp.

The state is backlogged with criminal cases, and the easiest and cheapest method of disposing of them is to get the suspect to plead guilty to a lesser charge than the original one. The defendant gets a shorter sentence, and the state gets away with having a fifteen-minute trial, with no jury. Everybody's happy, right?

Wrong. And there's plenty you can do about

it. In the first place, no one should ever plead guilty to a charge he is innocent of. Even if he is found guilty, the innocent plea will always be on the record and the case can be reopened later in the event new evidence comes to light.

Secondly, get rid of the public defender. There is absolutely no excuse for a public defender to give you this kind of runaround. Half of these guys are conscientious and helpful; the other half couldn't care less. You obviously have a bad one. Get in touch with Legal Aid or the American Civil Liberties Union and ask for help.

What kind of treatment can a teenager expect if he is arrested?

Being arrested is an experience everyone should be required to undergo at the age of fourteen or so. It would put an end to crime. First of all, the teenager is searched on the street, then handcuffed and put in the back of a police car. The handcuffs just might be a little tight, but don't bother complaining. The back seat of the police car will have no door handles which is a good indication of what is to come. From that point on, someone else will open doors for him, tell him when to sit, when to walk, and whether or not he can use the toilet.

Once at the station, a policeman will remove the teenager's belt, shoe laces, and everything from his pockets. Chances are, he will not be allowed to smoke, and if he is, he'll have to get a light from a policeman.

After being photographed and fingerprinted, he will be thoroughly searched. This search could be a simple "frisk" or a more involved "skin search." A skin search requires the prisoner to strip completely and be examined minutely by a policeman. The officer will wear rubber gloves—he will not be gentle. Young ladies need not feel that they will be excluded from this type of search. They get a matron to perform it on the girls. She isn't gentle either, and the search often includes a complete pelvic examination.

This concludes the booking process. If there is a juvenile hall, teenagers are transferred there. If not, they are sometimes locked in a room or a cell. If the kid happens to be over eighteen, he's thrown in a cell. A kid picked up on a traffic warrant could easily find himself in the company of robbers, murderers, and sexual perverts.

After that, there's nothing. For hours at a time, nothing. Days are broken up by feeding periods which usually occur at six in the morning and four in the afternoon. No menus.

There's plenty of time to sleep on a single bunk, possibly without a mattress. One blanket, no pillow. The worst part of it is the noise. Jails are never silent. Bars clang, men scream, toilets flush automatically every five minutes. Those toilets are right out in the open and don't have seats on them.

Twenty-four hours in jail seems like months, seventy-two hours, a lifetime. A prisoner feels as though he's been reborn when released. Jails are designed to be unpleasant as a deterrent to crime. For the average person they do the job.

What can a teenager expect to find in a camp?

Camp isn't as bad as jail, but it's not the Boy Scouts either. Most youth camps are work camps, and the work could range from hauling manure on a pig farm to fighting fires. A youth camp offers advantages over jail. Some have recreation rooms, where inmates can write letters, read, play ping-pong, sometimes shoot pool, as well as libraries and arts and crafts facilities.

The day is long and hard, and if the recreation room is used at all, it is because the inmate has had time to build up his stamina. For the first few weeks, he will come in after work and pass out without even bothering to shower. There are other problems too. Homosexuality is not unknown in camps, and, of course, there is always a leader and his gang to contend with.

My son has been told that if he is convicted for the burglary charge he is facing, he will probably be assigned to a youth training school. Is there an advantage in this?

Yes and no. A training school does provide the inmate the opportunity to learn a trade, but the facility itself is a lot closer to a prison than a camp. The inmate is supposed to be trained to be a skilled workman when he gets out, but he doesn't have any choice as to what trade he'll learn. Homosexuality and violence seem to be more prevalent in a training school than a camp, even though some schools are located in college campus type settings. Given a choice, I'd take camp.

My daughter came home last night stoned out of her mind. I want the guy who gave her the dope. Who do I see?

The local vice-narcotics department of the police. However, there is nothing the police can do if your daughter won't give you the person's name. By the way, don't assume automatically it was the boyfriend. Girls pass along drugs, too.

Are there ways for concerned parents to work with the police to stop trouble before it starts?

Definitely. The police in most areas would like nothing better than to help keep kids out of trouble. In Los Angeles, there is a program called the Basic Car Plan. This arrangement gives the community as a whole a chance to know and better understand its police department. The officers hold monthly meetings in a school auditorium or civic building at which they show films explaining law and police procedures, demonstrate the latest equipment and cover subjects like rape prevention and first aid, answer questions and discuss community problems. The majority of the communities involved have been enthusiastic.

Another great program is the Ride Along. In this program a teenage student spends several hours with on-duty policemen in a patrol car. It gives the kids a chance to talk at length with policemen as fellow human beings and to understand the strain involved in their demanding jobs. It also gives the cops a chance to become better acquainted with the kids. Knowing each other as Charles Smith, student, and John Brown, policeman, does a lot to remove the "pig" and "punk" stereotypes.

Danny Thomas has been developing a program in which policemen and students play an annual football game—the Pigs versus the Freaks. The participants get enthusiastically involved with the game, which is followed by a picnic for all their families. It would be easy to start such a program, and there's no reason it has to be limited to football once a year. There's also baseball, basketball, and volleyball.

The purpose of all these programs is to bring parents, teenagers, and police together to promote understanding of mutual problems. This alone does much to combat trouble before it starts. See your local police department, and get the ball rolling.

CONCLUSION

Being a teenager, as we all know, is not the easiest time of life. Every painful emotion, every problem is being experienced for the first time, is entirely unique, so the teenager feels. I'm sure there are few of us who wouldn't trade the hassles of inflation, budgets, raising children, and just plain surviving in the adult world for those balmy days of dreams and heartbreaks we experienced as adolescents, but those problems seemed insurmountable at the time.

Not one of us can completely understand someone else. It is especially difficult when at least three decades of experience separate most parents from their teenagers. We might be able to identify with their youth, but without living through it, our understanding of it will always be colored by our own adolescent experience. And today's society is quite a leap from that of the forties and fifties.

The blame for the lack of communication between parents and teenagers has been placed on the generation gap, not without basis. The young man in 1942 was ready and willing to fight a war against tyranny and persecution. The young man in 1969 was not so willing to risk his life in a "limited advisory action" in Viet Nam. It's difficult for the father who patriotically fought in the Pacific to understand why his eighteen-year-old son wouldn't be willing to do the same in Southeast Asia. And the young man of 1969 doesn't understand why his father doesn't understand.

Similarly a parent may sympathize with the use of alcohol, but resist any discussion of drugs; may sentimentally recall zoot suits and bobby socks, but be outraged by long hair; may reminisce about dormitory raids, but put down rock festivals.

Understanding is the first step toward relating to another person. You don't have to speak another person's language; you don't have to have the same experiences, if you can speak to his or her feelings and emotions.

Communication is ninety percent listening, empathizing, and learning.

When my brother taught me leather craft, he showed me how to cut and assemble the strips of leather to make purses and belts, and then made me show him how to do it. From this intimate exchange, not only did I learn a skill, but both of us learned something about each other through a shared experience. It works the same way for parents and teenagers.

Everybody needs understanding and needs to belong. Whether a teenager gets this support from his parents, close relatives, from drug users, gangs, or weird antisocial groups will depend upon the home environment.

The problems of raising a family—the stress, the time taken up by the details of living, the tight finances—take a lot out of parents. Even if there isn't much time to spend together in organized family activities, there should be some family communication, if only a few minutes out of every day. Bringing the family together for at least one meal a day in which each member's plans and problems are discussed will make a world of difference in the long run.

Talk is what it is all about. If parents generate the kind of atmosphere in which a boy can discuss using drugs or a girl can discuss whether or not to sleep with her boyfriend, the parents will at least know what their children are thinking about. Most parents are quite shocked when their kids get into trouble. If a parent is aware of a potential problem, he can take steps to help the kid understand his position and the possible consequences of his actions.

A family has to work at communication. It doesn't occur overnight, although sometimes the shock of seeing a teenager in trouble is enough to open up the lines of communication. It's never too late for honesty and love to make a difference in a person's life.

This book has presented a variety of situations and methods of coping with problems. If I had to sum it all up, I'd repeat: Keep the channels of communication open, maintain your integrity, without giving in to the impulse to preach, and love the kid one hell of a lot.

There is an old and sometimes laughed at cliche: The family that prays together, stays together. This doesn't mean regular attendance at a church or synagogue.

Prayer is the sharing of gratitude, desires, fears, and love. A family sharing these feelings will build a close bond. For most of us, there is some higher power, something bigger than ourselves, whether it be a God, the spectacular forces of nature, or the intrinsic goodness of mankind. The shared belief in human love and a higher power can bring a family closer together than anything else.

INDEX